CATHOLIC
PRAYER BOOK

© Wyatt North Publishing, LLC 2014

About Wyatt North Publishing

Starting out with just one writer, Wyatt North Publishing has expanded to include writers from across the country. Our writers include college professors, religious theologians, and historians.

Wyatt North Publishing provides high quality, perfectly formatted, original books.

Send us an email and we will personally respond within 24 hours! As a boutique publishing company we put our readers first and never respond with canned or automated emails. Send us an email at hello@WyattNorth.com, and you can visit us at www.WyattNorth.com.

Foreword

This book features over fifty of the most popular Catholic prayers and an introduction to Catholic prayer by Jeremiah Vallery.

Enjoy an electronic database of traditional Catholic prayers for multiple occasions including Morning Prayer, Evening Prayers, Prayers at Mass, Prayers for Holy Communion, The Stations of the Cross, and more.

About the Author

Jeremiah Vallery is a Ph.D. candidate in Systematic Theology at Duquesne University and an adjunct professor at the University of St. Thomas in Houston, Texas. He received his M.A. in Theology and his B.A. in Philosophy and Theology from Ave Maria University. His dissertation topic is the cosmic soteriology of Benedict XVI and its relevance for the ecological crisis. Currently, he is working on paraphrasing and editing academic books for a Messianic Jewish nonprofit organization, tutoring a handful of students, and teaching at the University of St. Thomas. He lives in Spring, Texas with his wife and two daughters.

Introduction to Catholic Prayer

What is Prayer?

At its most basic level, prayer is an act whereby human beings communicate with a divine, superhuman being on whom they are dependent (R. Arbesmann). For the typical person living in pre-modern (especially pre-Enlightenment) times, prayer was something that seemed natural and understandable enough; the existence of supernatural beings was taken for granted, and most people considered praying to the gods and other celestial beings to be a necessity in a world fraught with uncertainties. Before the advent of Christianity, the world was perceived as a place shrouded in mystery, inhabited by a combination of gods, spirits, angels, demons, nymphs, and other beings.

Such a worldview seems rather archaic and naïve to many people in today's world. In their view, with the rise of scientific knowledge, all of the mysterious aspects of the world seem to have been explained away, and human beings no longer seem to have any need of the supernatural.

Despite this process of what has been termed "demythologization," religion continues to be a powerful force in contemporary society. Joseph Ratzinger (Benedict XVI) explains why this is the case in his classic theology book *Introduction to Christianity*. While science is able to describe how things are, it is incapable of explaining why they are and what we should do. By its nature, science deals with calculating thought, not reflective thought. Science can explain how nuclear weapons work but cannot tell us whether they should be used. The ambivalence of technology highlights the necessity of deriving one's moral compass from philosophy and religion (66-74).

Prayer is a ubiquitous element of every religion, whether it takes the form of the *shema* in Judaism, the call to prayer in Islam, the Lord's Prayer in Christianity, or meditative practices in Eastern religions. In all of these religions, the function of prayer is to bring the religious devotee to a state of greater perfection. In some of these religions, however, prayer is not directed to a "thou," but instead takes the form of meditative practices in which the ultimate goal is to realize that *atman* (the individual soul) is *brahman* (the world soul). By contrast, in the three great monotheistic religions, prayer is always addressed to a "thou," namely God, who is one, and who is fundamentally distinct from the world. In the monotheistic religions, prayer is essentially a kind of communication between an individual and God.

There are certain schools in Christian thought, especially in the East, which teach that through accepting Jesus Christ, becoming more virtuous, and communicating with God through prayer and the sacraments, an individual is able to go through a process of apotheosis. In the West, this process is called deification. Essentially, this transformative process makes the individual like God and enables the Christian to enter into a mystical union with God; however, the ontological difference between God and human beings is never actually overcome, even when an individual enters heaven. Yet the goal of deification is for Christians to become like God inasmuch as human beings are capable of becoming like him. According to St. John of the Cross, in heaven the souls of the saints are assimilated to God and are "God by participation" (377).

Christian prayer has been defined as "the filial expression of one's desires for self and others to the heavenly Father from whom come all good things, natural or supernatural" (Kennedy and Pennington). The saints have defined prayer in various ways. St. Thérèse of Lisieux, for instance, describes prayer as "an aspiration of the heart ... a simple glance directed to heaven ...a cry of gratitude and love in the midst of trial as well as joy ...which expands my soul and unites me to Jesus" (242). Similarly, St. John Damascene calls prayer the lifting up of the soul to God and the asking of good things from God (*The Orthodox Faith*, 3.24). These descriptions of prayer are combined in the following definition: "an elevation of our soul to God to offer Him our homage and ask His favors, in order to grow in holiness for His glory" (Tanquerey, para. 501).

The most distinctive characteristics of Catholic prayer are (1) it is a form of communication between an "I" and a "thou," (2) the 'thou' to whom the prayer is addressed is either God, the Blessed Virgin Mary, or one (or more) of the saints, and (3) the address must be reverent. As we have already seen, Catholic prayer must be addressed to someone. Ultimately, all prayers are directed to God, as will become clear below. Catholic prayer is different from Eastern meditative practices, which focus on the self and the energy of the world since those forms of prayer do not extend to the creator. Catholic prayer is always a personal activity since the individual who prays, even if he or she is praying a kind of meditative prayer in which the focus is on the presence of God, is ultimately striving to become more like God and is seeking to communicate with the Lord.

If prayer is not communication between a Christian and God or one of the saints, then it is not truly Christian prayer. While one may be speaking to a holy individual, if the individual has not been declared to be officially holy (i.e., canonized, beatified, etc.), then such an address cannot be considered a prayer. Moreover, since one of the requirements for beatification and canonization is that a person must have already completed the course of his or her earthly life, no form of address to a living person, however holy, can be considered a prayer. A person speaking to the pope, for instance, is not praying. Christian prayer is always directed ultimately to God, whether it is a direct address to one or all of the persons of the Trinity or a request to one or more of the angels and saints for intercession. In the latter case, the angels and saints would be acting as intermediaries between the one who prays and God.

A Catholic who merely thinks about good things or is caught up in contemplating the beauty of the world is not truly praying unless he or she is lifting up his or her heart to God. Simply having a good feeling or being lost in wonderment is not the same thing as praying. Although religions such as Buddhism may allow for an abstract contemplation bereft of any subject or theme, such an abstract schema of prayer is absent in the Christian tradition. Even the type of prayer advocated by the *Cloud of Unknowing*—a thirteenth-century text written by a British monk, which maintains that clearing one's mind is the perfect way to dispose oneself to prayer and to unite oneself to God—has God as the ultimate goal of prayer. This type of prayer is characterized by the conviction that God exists and that the Catholic Church teaches the truth. When one uses this method of prayer, one is placing oneself in the presence of God; and in this way it is not abstract, but concrete.

Communication need not be vocal all the time. Sometimes, being in the presence of another is enough to express love, fidelity, and gratitude. In this sense, prayer can be considered as communion with the triune God. When one places oneself in God's presence, one is drawing nearer to his or her creator and redeemer. The *Catechism of the Catholic Church* explains that this possibility of communion with God derives from Baptism, which brings Christians into a special unity with Christ. "Prayer is Christian insofar as it is communion with Christ and extends throughout the Church, which is his Body," teaches the Catechism. "Its dimensions are those of Christ's love" (para. 2565).

The Kinds of Prayer

There are many kinds of prayer—vocal, mental, liturgical, devotional, and mystical, for instance. In general, prayer can be categorized according to its purpose, addressee, context, and position on the vocal-mental spectrum.

First of all, prayer may be divided according to its purpose. Traditionally, there are four purposes of prayer, which are encapsulated by two popular acronyms, (1) PART (Petition, Adoration, Reparation, and Thanksgiving) and (2) ACTS (Adoration, Confession, Thanksgiving, and Supplication). Both acronyms share adoration and thanksgiving as divisions of prayer; they differ in the other sets of terms—that is, in petition/supplication and reparation/confession.

Through adoration, the one who prays glorifies God above all things and admires God's attributes. This form of prayer is also known as worship or praise. The one who worships God praises him as the supreme being and recognizes his awesomeness and majesty as the source of all things. This kind of prayer implies that God is a personal God and not some deity in the heavens who, like Aristotle's God, is incapable of communicating with human beings. Deists generally are not accustomed to adoration of God, even though they often admire the divine handiwork of creation. If God does not communicate with humanity, it makes little sense to adore and worship him; but if he is capable of communicating with us, adoration becomes not only possible but also necessary.

Thanksgiving is naturally related to adoration since the one who glorifies God sees God at work in his or her life. In addition to this, adoration and thanksgiving are complementary since the one who worships and praises God adores him and his attributes, thereby praising him for his being, whereas the one who thanks God is thanking him for what he has done or what he has given. All good things, whether they are inherent in God's being or flow from God's being, come from God. Thanksgiving not only implies thanksgiving for God's blessings in this life but also implies an entrustment to divine providence, which is especially necessary in the midst of the vicissitudes of life.

Petitionary prayer is prayer that is directed toward God and seeks something from him. In other words, it is spoken by one who experiences a particular need. This type of prayer is the prayer of a trustful child who asks his parents for good things. While God knows all, he still desires that we ask him for things. The best way to think about the prayer of supplication is to imagine a small, needy toddler. Of course, if the toddler's parents are good parents, they will give the child the things she needs. The child does not need to ask her parents for them, but if the toddler recognizes her neediness, she is often more thankful when she gets what she asked for than if she had asked for anything in the first place. The same idea can be applied to us: while we do not need to ask God for anything in order for him to give us the things that we need, he wants us to ask him for good things. God responds to our wants when we pray in the same way that a parent would respond: he either grants what we wish, delays giving to us what we ask of him, or does not grant us what we wish because it is not good for us or there is something better in store for us.

In the prayer of reparation and confession, the individual recognizes that he or she has committed sin; confesses that sin; and asks God for forgiveness. This type of prayer is necessary for every Catholic. Although the baptized are cleansed from original sin and all personal sin at Baptism, the effects of original sin remain. One of the effects of original sin is a tendency to sin, which is called concupiscence. This weakness makes it easy for human beings to fall into sin. Since everyone sins at certain points in life, it is imperative to seek God's forgiveness and to turn away from sin. This form of prayer is especially connected to the sacraments of Penance (or Reconciliation) and Anointing of the Sick. The Catholic Church teaches that while God is able to forgive our sins if we are truly repentant, this does not mean that we do not have to confess our mortal sins in the sacrament of Reconciliation.

Prayer can be divided according to whether it is addressed to God, the Blessed Virgin Mary, or the saints. Prayer that is directed toward God, especially prayer that pertains to worshipping and adoring him, is called *latria* while prayer that is addressed to the angels and saints is called *dulia*. Latria is essentially worship of the Godhead while dulia is honor that is given to a saint. Prayer directed to the saints is always intercessory prayer since adoration, thanksgiving, and confession are reserved for God. Of course, in one's prayer to a saint, one can mention one's sins, thank the saint for his or her prayers, and admire his or her good qualities, just as one might do in conversation with a friend; but only God can forgive sins, and he alone is worthy of our highest thanks and praise.

Prayer addressed to the Blessed Virgin Mary is called *hyperdulia*. The reason why Catholics honor the mother of Christ is because Mary was kept free from original sin and avoided all personal sin during her earthly life. Of course, this is what the doctrine of the Immaculate Conception, proclaimed by Pius IX in 1854, teaches. In addition, by virtue of the hypostatic union—i.e., the union of the human and divine natures in Jesus—Mary is the mother of God (*theotokos*). Hyperdulia is far above the honor given to the rest of the saints because Mary is the most perfect creature whom God has ever created, but the honor that is given to her is of a totally different nature than the worship that is given to God; in other words, the difference is not a difference of degree, but a difference of kind. Catholics honor Mary above every other creature, but they do not worship her.

Prayer is also divided according to its context. The two most general contexts of prayer are liturgical, or the public prayer of the Church, and devotional, or personal prayer. There are also a number of prayers—such as morning prayers, evening prayers, prayers before and after meals, and prayers for special occasions—that are intended to be prayed in specific contexts, but all of the prayers that are said in these contexts can be categorized as either liturgical or personal prayer. Liturgical prayer includes not only the prayer of the Mass, which is the greatest of all prayers, but also the Liturgy of the Hours and prayers addressed on certain occasions, such as the prayers said by a priest at a house blessing.

Finally, prayer can be categorized according to where it falls on the vocal-mental spectrum. The most basic form of prayer is vocal. While vocal prayer can sometimes be expressed in one's own words to God, it often is expressed in forms that are traditionally set, such as the Our Father and the Hail Mary. Vocal prayers can be private, communal, or public. They are private when they are said alone, communal when they are prayed in a group, and public when they meet the following conditions: (1) "use of an approved formula," (2) "recitation in the name of society, which for the Christian is the Church," and (3) "legitimate delegation." It follows that members of the clergy and religious who recite the Divine Office, even alone, are offering public prayer (Kennedy and Pennington). The public prayer of the Church, which is always considered liturgical, is vocal in nature.

When one prays without using words, such prayer is called mental prayer. This type of prayer is divided into formal and diffused prayer. The former is the kind of mental prayer that takes place in the context of an allotted time, specifically set aside for this sort of activity, whereas the latter is mental prayer that one offers to God while one goes about performing his or her daily tasks.

Formal mental prayer may be discursive, affective, or contemplative. Discursive prayer is also called meditation and primarily consists of considerations, reasoning, affections, and resolutions. During meditation, a particular sacred event is often pondered by the one who prays. Generally speaking, meditation on the event should, ideally, lead to holy affections and finally to firm resolutions, although it is not necessary that specific resolutions follow every single meditation.

Affective prayer lies between discursive and contemplative prayer. In this form of prayer, the affections prevail while formal considerations recede into the background. Because the affections experienced in this type of prayer are multifaceted, it does not achieve the simplicity of contemplative prayer, which rests in God alone.

Contemplative prayer is divided into acquired contemplation (active contemplation) and infused contemplation (passive contemplation, or mystical prayer). Acquired contemplation "is the simple gaze upon God as known through faith and experienced through love" (Aumann) while infused contemplation is an experiential knowledge of God in which the one who prays feels united with God. Infused contemplation is the goal of mystical theology, which culminates in what St. John of the Cross calls the mystical marriage.

The Rosary is a hybrid of vocal and mental prayer. As one prays the series of Our Fathers, Hail Marys, and Glory Bes, one meditates on different events in the life of Christ and of the Blessed Virgin Mary. The Rosary is an example of devotional prayer and should not be considered as a liturgical prayer. While the Rosary is a very important devotion and one that is easy to learn, the liturgical prayers of the Church are more significant than the Rosary because the liturgy is the official prayer of the Bride of Christ addressed to the Bridegroom.

A Brief History of Prayer, Part I: Prayer Before the Advent of Christianity

Prayer is a remarkably human phenomenon. While it is true that some domesticated animals have been trained to be extremely loyal companions to human beings (e.g., dogs), prayer is something that is different from the attitudes that animals show to humans and to other animals. After all, while dogs want attention, enjoy company, and often manifest tenacious loyalty, they do not build temples, see human beings as the end all of their existence, or meditate religiously on their masters. While some dog lovers might beg to differ, dogs do not treat us as if we were gods.

In contrast, human beings have always had a tendency to look above them, not only for their physical necessities in life but also to satisfy their need for meaning. This is inextricably connected to the human capacity for reason. It is also tied to metaphysics since man has always sought an explanation for the existence of the universe.

For as long as the human race has existed, human beings have prayed. The rise of cults inevitably followed the rise of civilizations, in part because such cults were often funded by those in political power. In ancient civilizations, the relationship between human beings and the gods was conceived as a mutually dependent cycle: people would offer the gods sacrifices, and the gods, being pleased, would bless them with good things such as fruitful harvests, children, fair weather, and protection from enemies. The mythologies woven by poets partially satiated man's desire for an explanation of his world. One of the main problems with the cosmogonists' description of the world's creation and of the gods is that the gods they depicted were all too human and did not convey the grandeur and majesty of a supreme being. Greek philosophy from Socrates to Aristotle shattered this illusion, even though these philosophers were fond of mythology and often used mythological stories to explain elements of their philosophies.

In addition to dismantling the claims of polytheism, some of the foremost Greek philosophers signaled a remarkable shift, namely the shift from prayer performed with ulterior or overt, materialistic motives to a more spiritually motivated form of prayer. Socrates, for instance, prays for "inward beauty" and recognizes the greatness and unity of the divine (Arbesmann). Recognizing that prudence, temperance, fortitude, and justice are necessary virtues for human beings, Socrates sought a more divine life than his predecessors did; and while Aristotle does not view prayer as becoming for human beings, his theory of virtue as expressed in his *Ethics* significantly impacted Western thought on virtue via the writings of St. Thomas Aquinas.

The development of monotheism marked a watershed in ancient biblical times. Instead of believing in a whole pantheon of quarreling, jealous, and competing gods, Israel recognized only one God. The effect this had on prayer is that faithful Israelites addressed their prayers only to Yahweh, and all other gods that had been recognized in the past were demoted. Yahweh was deemed as having supreme dominion over all of the earth and as being the creator of all things.

With the mingling of the Greek philosophical stream and the Jewish monotheistic stream in the Hellenized world after the conquests of Alexander the Great in the fourth century BC, it occurred to people at the time that the God of Israel could be described in philosophical categories. The Wisdom of Solomon (second to first century BC) and the writings of Philo of Alexandria (c. 20 BC – c. AD 50) bear the stamp of Hellenism. One of the effects of this encounter between the Greek and Jewish world is that monotheism no longer remained merely a theological assertion, but became a rationally defensible position.

There were many forms of prayer in ancient Israel, but the most important ones were the prayers associated with the Temple cult. The Israelites offered animal sacrifices to Yahweh. They also prayed the psalms, which many theologians believe were liturgical texts designed to be prayed on certain occasions. In addition to these prayers, there existed what have been termed the Old Testament sacraments. Circumcision was the initiation ceremony in which a male was incorporated into the people of Israel. Animal sacrifices were offered on behalf of the people by the levitical priests. All of these prefigure the sacraments that exist in the Catholic Church today.

Another watershed moment in the history of prayer was the Babylonian exile following the destruction of the Temple by the Babylonians in 586 BC. At first glance, this cataclysmic event might not seem to have much significance for the development of prayer among the people of Israel; however, this exile was the catalyst of a great maturation process. Whereas before, the people of Israel had relied on the sacrifices offered on the altar in the Temple, now they were forced to cope without a Temple and had to learn how to foster and maintain a personal relationship with God without the Temple cult. More attention was given to meditation on the words of the prophets and on prayer in secret. In fact, it was during this time that synagogues developed (Abrahams). Even as the Jews were enabled to return to Jerusalem and rebuild the Temple under the decree of Cyrus the Great in 539 BC, they retained their newly found wisdom and learned to incorporate the Scriptures into their spiritual lives.

Another effect of the exile was the termination of the Davidic dynasty. Although the people were acutely aware that the psalms promised that David would have a son on his throne forever, post-exilic Israel had no Davidic king. Instead, Israel was under the dominion of the Medes and Persians, the Greeks, and finally the Romans, who ultimately destroyed Jerusalem in AD 70. Immediately before the time of Christ, Messianic expectations were high because of the disparity between the prophecies in the Tanakh (the Hebrew Scriptures) and the political situation.

This form of expectation prepared the people of Israel for the coming of Jesus. Such hope, when it was exercised in a nonradical (i.e., in contrast to the zealots) and spiritual form, was the Jewish analogue to the Christian theological virtue of hope. This is why Simeon, expressing his joy at the fulfillment of the hope of his people after having seen the infant Jesus, could pray, "Now, Master, you may let your servant go in peace, according to your word, for my eyes have seen your salvation, which you prepared in sight of all the peoples, a light for revelation to the Gentiles, and glory for your people Israel" (Luke 2:29-32, New American Bible).

A Brief History of Prayer, Part II: Christian Prayer from the First to Twelfth Centuries

The incarnation, death, and resurrection of Jesus Christ inaugurated a new era of prayer. Now all prayer was to be directed to God through Jesus, the great high priest and mediator between God and human beings. Since in his person, Jesus is the *shekinah* (the presence of God), he took the place of the Temple (cf. John 2:19-22). Because Jesus is the perfect revelation of the Father, and he and the Father are consubstantial, the one who approaches the altar and receives Jesus' body and blood is capable of achieving a profound intimacy with him and the Father. Of course, such intimacy is predicated on separation from deadly sins and presupposes a reformed life. This unprecedented closeness is a wonderful effect deriving from the hypostatic union of the human and divine natures in Jesus.

From the time of Jesus until today, there has been great continuity in the history of Christian prayer; at the same time, however, while Christian prayer has retained its roots and identity, it has accumulated various features and characteristics that reflect the idiosyncrasies of different historical eras. All authentically Christian prayer is one in light of the doctrine of the communion of saints, which highlights the immortal nature of the Catholic Church and indicates that although the Church exists in time, it also somehow transcends it.

Jesus set the tone for the entire history of Christian prayer, and for this reason Christian prayer remains profoundly Jewish in many respects. Jesus taught his disciples how to pray, giving them what has come to be known as "The Lord's Prayer" or the "Our Father" (Matt. 6:9-13; Luke 11:2-4). This prayer is remarkable for its brevity as well as its profundity. He also inaugurated the Mass by celebrating the Last Supper with his disciples. Jesus' many intimate prayers to the Father in the Gospels, often spoken in solitude, provide a model for all Christians to follow. Jesus also had an evident love of the Hebrew Scriptures, thus anticipating in his person the Church's devotion to the Word of God. All of these practices were continued by the early Church.

In the first millennium of Christianity, thought on prayer progressed in various stages. In the first stage, although prayer was often said spontaneously, it tended to be focused in a liturgical setting. During the first several centuries of the Church before the Edict of Milan in AD 313, liturgical rites were a closely guarded secret. In the middle of the second century, St. Justin Martyr (c. 100-165) outlined the basic structure of the Mass in his *First Apology* (67.3); but what exactly was said in these liturgies, other than the words of consecration, is not revealed. In other words, while liturgical texts from that period of time no longer exist, Justin's account describes the essential components of the Sunday liturgy. The basic arrangement of the Mass has remained the same for over 1800 years.

After the Edict of Milan, Christianity was embraced by Constantine and, eventually, by the Empire. The liturgical texts were preserved; Church histories were written; archaeological excavations became popular; and prayer flourished. The type of prayer that became popular at this time is related to the phenomenon of monasticism. Seeking to avoid the worldliness of Rome, Benedict of Nursia (480-543) established a monastery at Subiaco. In Benedict's view, a monk is one who devotes his entire life to prayer in communion with other like-minded individuals.

The Divine Office, also known as the Liturgy of the Hours, became embedded in the monastic lifestyle. This series of prayers was said at different times of the day and corresponded with different seasons. The practice of praying at various times of the day can be traced through apostolic times back to the time of the Babylonian exile, when synagogues first came into existence. The Jews prayed morning prayers and evening prayers to replace the morning and evening sacrifices that were mandated by the Torah (Exod. 39:28-29). In addition to morning and evening prayers, there were other natural times for prayer, such as nightfall; however, Jewish tradition stresses that every moment of the day is an acceptable time to pray and that praying seven times a day as mentioned in the psalms (Ps. 119:164) is to be taken metaphorically (Abrahams). The Christian monastic tradition, however, set up seven different times for prayer, thus taking the psalmist at his word. Nonetheless, like Judaism, Christianity holds that every moment is an acceptable time to lift up one's heart and mind in prayer to God.

In the West, Lectio Divina became a popular form of meditational prayer. Lectio Divina is a kind of meditative, prayerful reading of the Scriptures. As Benedict XVI pointed out, its beginnings can be traced to Origen of Alexandria, the great third-century biblical exegete ("Origen of Alexandria: The Thought [2]"). This method of reading the Scriptures is far more prayerful and personal than is academic, critical analysis of the Bible. The Fathers of the Church and early saints, including Ss. Ambrose, Augustine, Hilary of Poitiers, Benedict of Nursia, and Gregory the Great, continued this practice of Lectio Divina, and St. Benedict incorporated Lectio Divina into his Rule (#48). Lectio Divina was formalized by the Carthusian monk Guigo II in *The Ladder of Monks*. In this work, Guigo describes the stages of Lectio Divina as having four steps: a brief Scripture passage is (1) read, (2) mediated upon, (3) responded to in prayer, and (4) interiorized in quiet, contemplative stillness with God (81-82). Lectio Divina was heartily recommended by St. Bernard of Clairvaux. This practice is still important for Catholics today.

In the East, Hesychasm became popular. Hesychasm is a kind of prayer in which the one who prays repeats the Jesus Prayer—i.e., "Lord Jesus Christ, Son of God, Have mercy on me, a sinner"—while directing one's mind to God and concentrating on being in union with him. The praying person is expected to inhale while saying the first part of the prayer, then exhale while saying the second part of the prayer. In this way, the mind, body, and soul of the one who prays to God are all involved in a holy synergy directed toward God. This prayer is connected to the statement that no one can call Jesus "Lord" without the Holy Spirit (1 Cor. 12:3). It is thought that by praying the Jesus Prayer, the one who prays is disposing himself or herself to communion with the Holy Spirit. Hesychastic practices became embedded in Eastern monasticism, and Hesychasm is the primary method of prayer used by monks in the Orthodox churches today.

During this time, iconography emerged in the East. Iconography is a form of art that is closely related to prayer. The theology of iconography rests on the idea that the icons serve as windows into the supernatural world. The iconographer does not paint icons, but writes them. There is a regimen of fasting and prayer that the iconographer is supposed to observe before writing an icon. This art form is characterized by sobriety as opposed to the passionate expression of emotions in Baroque art. The nonrealistic depiction of the saints in icons conveys the sense that they exist in another world. Icons are meant to stir the heart and mind toward prayer; and since the majority of the figures depicted in icons are angels and saints, icons strengthen the sense of the communion of saints as well as the sense of continuity between the members of the Church in previous generations and those who are alive today. Icons serve as a reminder that in God's sight, all are alive (cf. Luke 20:38).

The great art form that developed in the West was Gregorian chant. The roots of Gregorian chant stretch back to biblical days, at least insofar as psalms were set to music. This kind of music is marked by a profound simplicity on account of its monophonic nature, and its sobriety in many ways parallels the sense of sobriety conveyed by icons. While Gregorian chant existed in the early Church, only in the ninth century did the chants begin to be written down (Saulnier, 7). Gregorian chant graced the liturgical services of Europe for centuries, and its melodies and content produced a prayerful environment in the Romanesque churches and Gothic cathedrals.

One of the most remarkable individuals during this period of time was St. Hildegard of Bingen (1098-1175), a Benedictine abbess, who was proclaimed a Doctor of the Church by Pope Benedict on October 7, 2012. Hildegard was a polymath; her various writings and artistic endeavors cover widely diverse topics such as mystical theology, poetry, music, illuminated manuscripts, and medicine. Her music is similar to Gregorian chant since it was monophonic, but her melodies had a much broader range. In addition to her musical and artistic interests, Hildegard was a mystic. She had many visions of God and wrote down her mystical experiences in three volumes: *Scivias*, *Liber Vitae Meritorum*, and *Liber Divinorum Operum*. In many ways, Hildegard exemplifies the best of Christian mysticism and creativity in this period of time.

A Brief History of Prayer, Part III: Christian Prayer from the Twelfth to Sixteenth Centuries

The twelfth and sixteenth centuries both were characterized by great reformers: St. Bernard of Clairvaux (1090-1153), St. Ignatius of Loyola (1491-1556), and Ss. Teresa of Ávila (1515-1582) and John of the Cross (1542-1591). This period of time spans the early Middle Ages to the Counter Reformation. Of course, there were many other great saints in between, such as St. Francis of Assisi (1181-1226) and St. Dominic (1170-1221) and their academic counterparts, namely St. Thomas Aquinas (1225-1274) and St. Bonaventure (1221-1274). During this age, the modern university was established, and it was theology that stood supreme as queen over all other branches of learning—including philosophy, which was considered its handmaid.

One of the great developments during this period was the formation of the Rosary. In *The Secret of the Rosary*, St. Louis de Montfort (1673-1716) recounts how the Rosary was given to St. Dominic in 1214 by Our Lady in his struggle with the Albigensians (18). This dramatized account describes how Our Lady appeared to St. Dominic with three angels in order to present him with the Rosary, which she described as a weapon and a battering ram to be used in spiritual warfare. She also called the Rosary the Angelic Psalter.

Why would Mary describe the Rosary as a Psalter? The Rosary, in its initial form before Bl. John Paul II's introduction of the Luminous Mysteries, consisted of 150 Hail Marys, not counting the initial three. These Hail Marys were interpreted as substituting for the 150 psalms in the Psalter. The psalms were the staple of prayer for monks for centuries, and this tradition of praying the psalms stretched back to the days of ancient Israel. Lay people, often illiterate and not having the luxury to pray all of the psalms that the monks did, were able to pray the Rosary instead.

The Rosary combines mental prayer and vocal prayer. As one prays the words of the Rosary, one meditates on one of the central mysterious events of the life of Christ or of the Blessed

Virgin Mary. In many ways, this form of prayer is similar to Hesychasm. Since its insemination, the Rosary has been an extremely popular form of prayer in the West.

The doctrine of indulgences developed in the early medieval period. The history of indulgences is rather ambivalent since cases can be made for their benefits and their abuses. Before getting into the history of indulgences, the theological concept of indulgences should be explained.

There is a rather profound theology behind the concept of indulgences, which rests on the understanding of the punishment due to sin. The Catholic Church teaches that although sins may be forgiven in their entirety, depending on the level of perfection of the penitent's contrition and charity, there may still be some temporal punishment that needs to be paid. In other words, while the offense is forgiven, and one receives God's sanctifying grace, there is still something that needs to be repaired. What is this something? This residual price the repentant sinner must pay has been described as a debt owed to God because one has caused harm.

Examples from human relations are often used to explain indulgences. If one were to borrow a tool and lose it, or accidentally damage it, and ask for forgiveness, the lender may forgive the borrower; yet, typically, the lender will require some sort of recompense. This analogy breaks down, however, on a number of different levels. First, this example is from human relations—God is omnipotent and needs nothing from us, even if we do wrong. So again, what is this residual punishment?

The Church teaches that an indulgence is the partial or full remission of the temporal punishment due to sin. While the sacraments of Baptism and Confession lead to the full forgiveness of sins, there remains temporal punishment that has to be paid. This punishment would be paid either in this life or in the next, in purgatory. Joseph Ratzinger provides a most ingenious explanation of the concept of purgatory in *Eschatology: Death and Eternal Life*, explaining that those who enter heaven need to be pure as God is pure and that if other people are still suffering on account of one's sins on earth, one cannot be truly happy (189). Purgatory is a place of purification, a kind of antechamber to heaven, in which the soul is prepared to meet its maker; indeed, the fire of purgatory is the Lord himself. The individual who enters into purgatory is touched by eschatological divine fire so as to become "capable of God" (230). From this perspective, an indulgence would be the lessening of the pain of this purifying fire, which is God himself. With this in mind, let us return to the late Middle Ages.

It is said that the practice of accepting donations for indulgences brought about many political benefits such as the building of cathedrals, the founding of universities, the establishment of hospitals, and the repair of bridges, and that in addition to these secular benefits, the preaching of indulgences provided opportunities for spiritual revivals, led to an increase in devotion among the people, and fostered solidarity between people in this world and those who had already passed from this life to the next. Unfortunately, there were also many abuses associated with the preaching of indulgences. In fact, as early as 1215, the Catholic Church condemned the abuses of indulgences that were present in the Church at the time (Palmer and Tavardi).

When Martin Luther became aware of a recently established practice of clerics selling indulgences in exchange for donations to papal building projects, he became irate. Of course, the Church has never held that one can buy one's way into heaven, but to the masses this practice was beyond doubt a scandal. After all, only the rich could afford to donate large sums of money to building projects; they were therefore the only ones who could afford to "purchase" these indulgences. This was one of the practices that infuriated the passionate young Martin Luther.

Much has changed since Luther's time. The selling of indulgences has ceased, and some of the customs associated with indulgences have changed, especially in regard to the specified length of time attached to partial indulgences. Whereas previously, particular prayers were marked with an indulgence of 100 days, 200 days, one year, etc., in the aftermath of the Second Vatican Council, prayers that have an indulgence associated with them are marked either as partial or plenary (Palmer and Tavardi).

The Catholic response to the Reformation was the Counter-Reformation. St. Ignatius of Loyola, the founder of the Jesuits, wrote a remarkable treatise on ascetical and mystical theology called *The Spiritual Exercises*. This work, along with the works of Ss. John of the Cross (*Dark Night of the Soul* and *Ascent of Mount Carmel*) and Theresa of Ávila (*Interior Castle*), are the classics of sixteenth-century Spanish mysticism. After the sixteenth century, new technologies and sciences propelled prayer in new directions.

A Brief History of Prayer, Part IV: Christian Prayer from the Seventeenth to Twenty-First Centuries

Prayer in the seventeenth century developed quite significantly as a result of three events, which originated in part before the seventeenth century: (1) the invention of the printing press, (2) the Protestant Reformation (and Catholic Counter-Reformation), and (3) the scientific revolution. These events led to a very turbulent but fruitful time in the history of humanity and of the Catholic Church.

The invention of the printing press made the Bible more accessible to ordinary people. While the Catholic Church was at first reluctant to have the Scriptures so accessible—since, in their view, the Bible could be easily corrupted—the ability of the printing press to transmit knowledge, especially scriptural knowledge among the people, eventually won the day. This was formally recognized in the teachings of the Catholic Church during the Second Vatican Council, when the Council Fathers warmly recommended the frequent reading of the Scriptures (*Dei Verbum* 25). In addition to increasing the accessibility of the Bible, the printing press heralded the coming of the devotional prayerbook. Among the most popular of these books was *Introduction to the Devout Life* by St. Francis de Sales, the bishop of Geneva, which enjoyed wide popularity.

The Counter-Reformation went into full swing with the flourishing of the Jesuits, who brought the Gospel to the New World. In the seventeenth century, the Jesuits were at the forefront of learning. In fact, the Jesuits became the stewards of the astronomical Observatory of the Roman College that was founded in the eighteenth century. Such a congenial relationship between faith and science had not always existed; only a couple of centuries before, the Vatican had censured Galileo Galilei for the way he presented his scientific method, ultimately placing him under house arrest. The Catholic Church, however, has always emphasized the complementarity between faith and reason, something that was most clearly expressed by St. Thomas Aquinas in the *Summa Theologica*.

The classical age of science, which was enamored with humanity's newfound capacity to control nature through reason, slowly gave way to Romanticism. Some great luminaries began to be weary of the incredible claims of science and the encroachment of technology upon the sacredness of nature. Romanticism emphasized the emotions and the heart over pure reason. Prayer began to emulate the characteristics of this movement. New prayers were composed with flowery verbal ornamentation, and the heart's role in prayer was emphasized. This can be seen especially in the writings of Bl. John Henry Newman (1801-1890) and St. Thérèse of Lisieux (1873-1897).

The twentieth century was plagued by two world wars, but it was also blessed with an abundance of saints. Perhaps the most worthy of mention in a discussion of prayer are St. Pio of Pietrelcina, a great advocate of the Rosary and the sacraments; St. Jose María Escrivá, founder of Opus Dei; and John Paul II, popularly known as John Paul the Great. In 2002 John Paul II introduced the five Luminous Mysteries to the devotion of the Rosary. The rationale behind this move was that the traditional fifteen mysteries of the Rosary only covered the mysteries of Jesus' childhood, passion, resurrection, ascension, and the other Glorious Mysteries, thereby completely bypassing his public ministry. The five Luminous Mysteries are (1) the Baptism of the Lord, (2) the changing of water into wine at the wedding feast of Cana, (3) Jesus' preaching of the kingdom of heaven and the call to repent, (4) the transfiguration, and (5) the institution of the Eucharist.

One of the most significant events that occurred in this period of time was the liturgical reform in the Second Vatican Council. *Sacrosanctum Concilium* permitted the Mass to be celebrated in the vernacular. This enabled people to pray the Mass in their own language rather than Latin. Much ink has been spilt on the debate between liturgical conservatives and progressives, and it is not my intention to settle the debate in this introduction. Suffice it to say that the liturgical reforms stemming from the

Second Vatican Council had some very good consequences, including an increase in the ability of the laity to participate in the Mass, but that the actual implementation of the reforms often led to a variety of liturgical abuses. In 2007, Pope Benedict XVI issued *Summorum Pontificum*, which enabled the Tridentine Mass to be celebrated as an extraordinary form of the Roman Rite. The Mass prayers in this prayerbook follow the *Novus Ordo* form of the Mass.

The history of prayer continues in the twenty-first century. The place of the *Novus Ordo* Mass is firm, although the extraordinary form of the Mass is gaining in popularity in certain traditional circles. With the election of Pope Francis in 2013, a new pontiff, who emphasizes the apostolic preaching and the simplicity of the teachings of Jesus, sits on the throne of Peter. Pope Francis' call to imitate the Lord will bring about a time in which Catholics are more aware of their calling to be in closer communion with God through prayer. This emphasis simultaneously highlights the origin of Christian prayer and its destiny.

What Western Society Thinks About Prayer

In Western society, different attitudes toward prayer exist, which can can be categorized into prayers that are positive, those that are neutral, and those that are negative and sometimes downright hostile.

The first attitude toward prayer that is found in Western society is positive. There exist many religions in the western world: Christianity, Judaism, Islam, Hinduism, Buddhism, Sikhism, and traditional Native Indian religions. Although there are significant differences between the theological and religious outlooks of these religions, all of these groups share in common the belief that prayer can and should be addressed to a being or beings that are higher than mankind, or at the very least that human beings should meditate so as to grow in perfection. Because of this, there exists in these religions a powerful and abiding humility. In all of these religions, man does not stand at the apex of the universe; rather, he is subordinated to the absolute. Religious people typically manifest positive attitudes toward prayer.

The second type of attitude exhibited in Western society concerning prayer is one of neutrality. Agnostics sometimes fall in this camp since they claim that it is impossible to know God and to know which religion is right, assuming that there is a correct religion in the first place. Other people who fall in this camp would not necessarily identify themselves as agnostics. Many people who are searching for religious truth are fascinated with meditative prayer. They tend to label themselves as "spiritual" but not religious, by which they mean that they do not believe in following organized religion. Many of these people believe in a higher power and therefore incorporate some kind of prayer rituals or meditative practices into their daily lives. Those who fall in this category are usually not familiar with the richness of Christian prayer and the possible heights that can be achieved through ascetical and mystical contemplative practices, which is one of the reasons why they often turn to Eastern practices instead.

Finally, the third type of attitude toward prayer that is prominent in Western society is unquestionably negative. While not every atheist shows antipathy toward prayer, many do. The coupling of scientific and technological advances with the cultural crisis called "postmodernity" that arose in the aftermath of World Wars I and II led to an increased rhetoric on the part of atheists and agnostics against religion in general and prayer specifically. One of the reasons why some people are against prayer is that they are against anything that has to do with religion; in their view, religion is merely a means for religious leaders to exercise power, and prayer is merely a superstitious ritual. The wars of religion that followed the Protestant Reformation caused many people to view religion as nothing more than an ideology with the potential for violence and fanaticism. It is unfortunate that for many, many centuries, the history of the human race has been fraught with religious wars stemming from doctrinal and political disputes. Of course, to gloss over these differences and pretend as though they do not exist would be a rather naïve, facile solution to the divergent views that often cause tension in the world. Religions, however, have positive elements, which should not be overlooked.

A word should be said about the relationship between Church and State, a perennial issue in the United States that has become an important issue in many other democratic societies as well. The separation of Church and State ought not to mean the separation of one's political life and one's religious life. The way in which the founders of the United States conceived of the separation of Church and State is that the State should not support one religious institution over another. The separation is not intended to be a psychological bifurcation in the minds of citizens but rather a separation of the government from religious affairs. Prayer will only be respected directly in proportion to the degree that religions are respected and religious people are allowed to worship as they see fit. In a democratic society, it is important to tolerate other religious beliefs so as to foster religious freedom. When the State infringes upon the rights of religious groups, however, and the political and philosophical ideologies of those in power are forced onto all citizens regardless of religious beliefs, religious freedom becomes jeopardized. Freedom of religion and freedom of conscience must be respected so that religion can be practiced without government interference.

As for the disparaging views toward prayer that exist in many Western societies, Catholics should not succumb to the spirit of the age by yielding to any of these negative sentiments, often founded on the premises that God does not exist and that we cannot have sure knowledge of the ultimate truth of reality. The Catholic Church takes a balanced view in its stance toward truth. On the one hand, the Catholic Church has received from the apostles the Deposit of Faith. As such, the Church has been entrusted with the fullness of the truth. At the same time, because members of the Church are finite creatures, there is no way for the Church to be cognizant of the entirety of the truth, which is by its nature infinite. The Church, however, through the work of its theologians, is constantly deepening its understanding of the truth. The Church, entrusted with the truth given by Christ, is called to offer prayers to God in thanksgiving for the salvation that it has received in Christ Jesus. Catholics should not worry about what the world thinks regarding prayer, since it is better to please God than to please men (cf. Acts 5:29, Gal. 1:10).

Arguments Against Prayer

In *The Feast of Faith* (18ff.), Joseph Ratzinger describes three arguments against prayer: (1) the rejection of God's existence, (2) the rejection of personality and freedom, and (3) the rejection of a God who is able to interact with the world. All of the negative attitudes against prayer can be traced to one of these three philosophical positions.

In the first place, if an individual rejects a metaphysical view of God and chooses to believe that he does not actually exist, to such an individual, prayer seems superfluous. If there is no "thou" to whom a prayer can possibly be addressed, what need is there of prayer? As Ratzinger explains, "For Christian faith it is essential that it is addressing the God who really exists, the creator of all things and the ground of all being, and that this God has spoken to us. To reject metaphysics is to reject creation and hence the Christian concept of God itself" (19). Interestingly, some atheists are open to meditative practices, but only insofar as these practices increase their wellbeing in this life. This kind of meditation sharply differs from Christian meditation, which is always related to God.

Similarly, those who reject personality and/or freedom are more inclined to reject prayer than those who believe in free will. With the rise in popularity of the idea that the universe is a place where outcomes are predetermined—a view that is closely allied to materialism—the efficacy of prayer increasingly has been called into question. If everything were matter in motion, prayer would not be capable of changing anything since everything would be destined to follow a predetermined path. In this way of thinking "a rationally constructed world is determined by rationally perceived causality," which means that "[i]f there is only *one* kind of causality, man too as a person is excluded and reduced to an element in mechanical causality, in the realm of necessity" (20). According to this view, intercessory prayer is a useless waste of time. It may be that deists and agnostics can still offer prayer to God in the form of acknowledging God's greatness and offering him praise, but in such a view, God simply does not direct the course of events and does not care for human needs. This view is closely related to the next, which considers the eternal realm to be a region that is hermetically sealed off from the temporal realm.

The final view that militates against regard for prayer as a worthwhile activity is the notion that God operates on a different level than the world does. Of course, the central idea of deism, which holds that God set the universe in motion as a clockmaker winds up a clock and lets it run, is closely related to this idea. In its more sophisticated form, this argument is a metaphysical contention against the ability of eternity to break into time. This was Aristotle's view. If God were wholly inaccessible to human beings, praying to God would be like trying to break through glass by blowing on it with a straw.

Arguments against prayer share one thing in common: the rejection of God and/or his image in human beings. In the first case, God's existence is denied; in the second, human freedom is rejected—the very same freedom that theologians attribute to the fact that human beings are made in the image and likeness of God. This view is closely related to materialism, which holds that everything is matter in motion. In this view, human beings are essentially animals, and there is nothing that essentially separates human beings from the other animals. To the contrary, human dignity is far higher than the animal plane, and our capacity for love, nobility, abstract thought, and intellectual prowess strongly suggests that there is more to the universe than matter. This philosophical reflection buttresses the testimony of Scripture, which indicates that God has made us in his image and likeness.

Ratzinger postulates that it is only the Christian Trinitarian conception of God that is capable of relating time with eternity; all other monotheistic conceptions of God fall flat on their faces (21). The only other kinds of religious views that could exist under this third argument against prayer are the Asiatic religions and a kind of pure religion in which the one who prays does so simply to elicit the best within the individual himself or herself. These religious views of prayer, however, do not do justice either to God's freedom and personality or to ours. Only Christianity holds the answer to the question of time and eternity, an answer that promises God's faithful ones a share in eternal life.

Every argument against prayer stems from one of three philosophical positions: atheism, the illusory nature of human freedom, or the inability of eternity and time to interact. However, each of these perspectives contains its own weaknesses. In the end, prayer is necessary. This is not some naïve notion; instead, it rests on profound philosophical, theological, and sociological insights.

A Defense of Prayer

Those who hold a neutral stance toward prayer often believe that prayer holds the potential for beneficial effects on the one who prays. Although this is certainly true, the view held by many that prayer merely has an effect on the individual is entirely off the mark. The weakness of their argument stems from one of several presuppositions. Atheists (who deny God's existence), deists (who deny that God concerns himself with the world), and agnostics (those who claim that it is impossible to acquire certain knowledge of God) are all bent against prayer to varying degrees. Prayer is not an exercise in navel gazing; it is a very serious endeavor. If God exists and cares about us, we have an obligation to pray to him. Of course, prayer has an effect on the individual who prays, but its effects are much more far-reaching than the individual level. While one might argue that the benefits of prayer extend to others simply because by praying we make ourselves into better individuals, this is only part of the picture. Recall that Christian prayer necessarily involves a "thou" to whom one is praying. It would be pointless to pray to God as a Christian if God did not actually exist. For this reason, the metaphysical stance that God exists is essential to Christian prayer. This prevents the Christian from praying for purely personal or sociological motivations, which would be separate from any consideration of God's existence.

This world needs prayer. There are three primary kinds of relationship that benefit from prayer. The first such kind of relationship is between God and humanity; this vertical relationship is the most immediate one that is affected by prayer. The second kind of relationship that prayer cultivates is a horizontal relationship—for instance, between the members of the Body of Christ or between the Body and all humanity. Finally, the last kind of relationship that exists is one of mediation—that is, the relationship that humanity has with the rest of the world.

One must have a relationship with God in order to be saved, a relationship that may be called vertical insofar as God stands ontologically above us. Prayer is a means whereby an individual grows in one's relationship with Jesus Christ, the Savior. Without acquiring and fostering an intimate relationship with Jesus, one cannot be saved. (Of course, the theological asterisk that is always appended to this statement is that God has the power to save anyone who is inculpably ignorant of the truth and who desires to do what is necessary for salvation). Baptism is of no avail without such a relationship with Jesus; neither is faith alone since, as James says in his epistle, the devils believe but tremble with fear (James 2:19).

Secondly, prayer connects us with the other members of the Body of Christ and with the rest of humanity. When one has a relationship with Jesus through Baptism and faith, one becomes a member of the Church, the Bride of Christ, who is saved in its entirety. Salvation is a corporate affair. Prayer instills within us sentiments of good will toward the human race and helps us to realize that we are all connected on this earth. Prayer reminds Christians that they are members of the same Body of Christ and that they are called to cooperate so as to bring about a better world. This is closely connected with the doctrine of the communion of saints, which teaches that all members of Christ's Body, whether they are already in heaven, still on earth, or being purified in purgatory, are all interconnected.

The last reason why Christian prayer is so important for the world is that through prayer we act as intermediaries between God and the world. Not only is God the creator of the universe but he is also its redeemer. He governs all things according to his providence. Christians are capable of cooperating with God's providence through a prayerful disposition. In fact, through prayer, Christians are disposing themselves to become channels of God's grace and to help bring about his will on earth. It is only through an authentic relationship with the Father, the Son, and the Holy Spirit that Christians can hope to achieve this marvelous vocation to be active participants in

God's providence. In prayer, one becomes more connected to the rest of creation. By drawing near to the creator, one draws near to the font of being itself.

Another consideration complements this, namely that the one who prays and turns to God is directed toward him rather than away from him. Other creatures are amoral because they lack reason and because of this, it is impossible for them to be immoral – they are simply amoral creatures. While animals do not have the capacity to turn away from their creator, human beings do. Our freedom and reason are so powerful that we can turn away from the source of our own being. As such, prayer is what brings us in line with the rest of creation. By prayer, we participate in the bringing about of a transformation that begins with us and trickles down to the rest of creation, until God brings about a new heavens and a new earth (Rev. 21:1).

Prayer is a transformative practice. The one who prays becomes more conformed to Christ, and those who are conformed to Christ are capable of making a profound positive impact on humanity, the rest of our world, and human history.

Introductory Remarks about this Prayerbook

In this final chapter, I would like to describe the prayerbook that follows. First, I will elaborate upon the main features of the book. After this, I will discuss an editorial issue that I encountered when editing the manuscript of prayers. Third, I will describe the intended audience for this prayerbook. Finally, I will give instructions and suggestions on how to use this book.

The main features of this prayerbook are its fidelity to the Tradition of the Catholic Church on the one hand and its reflection of recent developments within the Catholic Church on the other. This prayerbook contains timeless prayers, which enable the one who is praying to reach back in time and pray with the early Church. It is characterized by an attention to the Tradition of the Catholic Church, which binds every age and every member of the Body of Christ together. This feature instills the prayerbook with a sober traditional element, which anchors it to the apostolic age.

At the same time, this book reflects the important updates ushered in by the Second Vatican Council, such as the *Novus Ordo* Mass parts, the emphasis on participation during the Mass, and the correspondence of the contents of various prayers with the developments in theological doctrine from the chair of Peter for the last 50 years. Like the Catholic faith, this prayerbook is simultaneously ancient and new since its roots stretch back to apostolic times yet it is capable of speaking to people in today's world.

In relation to this last point, while I was editing this book, I was confronted with the editorial decision of whether to employ the so-called "Old English" (that is, early modern English) nomenclature—consisting of "thees," "thous," and "thys"—or to render these prayers into contemporary modern English. I decided that the best method was to take a middle road by keeping certain traditional prayers—such as the Lord's Prayer, the Hail Mary, the Prayer to St. Michael, and the Memorare—in their older forms while ensuring that other prayers were more linguistically up to date. I concluded that by taking this path, I would be able to keep some of the traditional trimmings of certain key Catholic prayers while avoiding an overly cumbersome rendition. My hope is that the final product is approachable for Catholics who are interested in growing in their prayer lives yet reflects the beauty of the more familiar forms of some of the traditional prayers. I believe that this was the right editorial approach in light of the twofold goal of preserving the ancient flavor of some of the prayers and using language that is accessible to people today.

This prayerbook is intended for Catholics who are adept at prayer and for neophytes alike. For the most part, this prayerbook was designed for lay Catholics—i.e., those who are members of the common priesthood according to their Baptism—although it should be noted that there is nothing about this book that would prevent seminarians, ordained priests, and religious from using it. In addition to containing numerous prayers, this prayerbook contains the preceding concise history of prayer in four chapters, as well as a description of the various types of prayer that have developed over the centuries. This introduction to the history of Catholic prayer is designed to be an aid to the beginner but also to be instructive for those who are advanced at prayer. The list of references and sources for further reading was included for the sake of providing Catholics with invaluable academic and religious sources, which would be able to assist them in acquiring more knowledge about Catholic prayer.

How should this prayerbook be used? There exist a variety of contexts in which this prayerbook would be helpful. Catholics will want to keep this prayerbook handy since they can use it for all sorts of occasions. It is useful for praying one's morning and evening prayers, for preparing oneself to receive the sacraments of Confession and holy Communion, for praying the Stations of the Cross, and for praying some of the most beautiful and moving prayers that Catholic saints have ever composed. It can be used at home and in church, in private or in group settings, and at various times during the day. One can also bring this book into an adoration chapel so as to have a collection of formulaic prayers that can be used as a launching pad for more meditative practices, such as the Rosary and Lectio Divina. In short, there is no context related to Catholic prayer in which this prayerbook would be inappropriate.

I would like to conclude this chapter with a prayer: Lord God, source of all goodness, may this prayerbook increase the devotion of your people, help them to foster their relationship with the Holy Spirit, and lead them closer to you through your son Jesus Christ, for the good of their souls and for the salvation of the world. Amen.

Traditional Prayers

The Lord's Prayer

OUR Father who art in heaven,
hallowed be thy name.
Thy kingdom come.
Thy will be done
on earth as it is in heaven.
Give us this day our daily bread,
and forgive us our trespasses,
as we forgive those who trespass against us,
and lead us not into temptation,
but deliver us from evil.
Amen.

Hail Mary

HAIL MARY, full of grace,
the Lord is with thee;
blessed art thou among women,
and blessed is the fruit
of thy womb, Jesus.
Holy Mary, Mother of God,
pray for us sinners now
and at the hour of our death.

Amen.

Sign of the Cross

In the Name of the Father, and of the Son, and of the Holy Spirit. Amen.

Glory Be

Glory be to the Father, and to the Son, and to the Holy Spirit, as it was in the beginning, is now, and ever shall be, world without end. Amen.

Apostles' Creed

I believe in God, the Father Almighty, Creator of heaven and earth, and in Jesus Christ, his only Son, our Lord, who was conceived by the Holy Spirit, born of the Virgin Mary, suffered under Pontius Pilate, was crucified, died and was buried; he descended into hell; on the third day he rose again from the dead; he ascended into heaven, and is seated at the right hand of God the Father almighty; from there he will come to judge the living and the dead. I believe in the Holy Spirit, the holy Catholic Church, the communion of saints, the forgiveness of sins, the resurrection of the body, and life everlasting.
Amen.

Act of Faith

O MY GOD, I firmly believe that you are one God in three divine Persons, Father, Son and Holy Spirit. I believe that your divine Son became man and died for our sins, and that he will come to judge the living and the dead. I believe these and all the truths which the holy Catholic Church teaches, because you have revealed them, who can neither deceive nor be deceived.

Act of Contrition

O MY GOD, I am heartily sorry for having offended you, and I detest all my sins because I dread the loss of heaven and the pains of hell; but most of all because they offend you, my God, who are all-good and deserving of all my love. I firmly resolve, with the help of your grace, to confess my sins, to do penance, and to amend my life. Amen.

Grace Before Meals

BLESS us,
O Lord,
and these your gifts,
which we are about to receive from your bounty.
Through Christ our Lord.

Amen.

Grace After Meals

We give you thanks for all your benefits, O Almighty God, who lives and reigns world without end. Amen. May the souls of the faithful departed, through the mercy of God, rest in peace. Amen.

Prayers to the Blessed Virgin Mary

Hail Holy Queen

HAIL holy Queen, Mother of mercy, hail our life, our sweetness and our hope. To thee do we cry, poor banished children of Eve; to thee do we send up our sighs, mourning and weeping in this valley of tears. Turn then, O most gracious advocate, thine eyes of mercy toward us, and after this our exile, show unto us the blessed fruit of thy womb, Jesus, O merciful, O loving, O sweet Virgin Mary. Amen.

Memorare

REMEMBER,
O most gracious Virgin Mary,
that never was it known that anyone who fled to thy
protection,
implored thy help, or sought thy intercession
was left unaided.
Inspired with this confidence,
I fly unto thee,
O Virgin of virgins, my Mother;
to thee do I come,
before thee I stand,
sinful and sorrowful.
O Mother of thy Word Incarnate,
despise not my petitions,
but in thy mercy hear and answer me.
Amen.

The Angelus

THE Angel of the Lord declared unto Mary.

R. And she conceived by the Holy Spirit.

V. Hail Mary, full of grace, the Lord is with thee. Blessed art thou among women, and blessed is the fruit of thy womb, Jesus.

R. Holy Mary, mother of God, pray for us sinners, now, and at the hour of our death. Amen.

V. Behold the handmaid of the Lord.

R. Be it done unto me according to thy word.

V. Hail Mary, full of grace, the Lord is with thee. Blessed art thou among women, and blessed is the fruit of thy womb, Jesus.

R. Holy Mary, mother of God, pray for us sinners, now, and at the hour of our death. Amen.

V. And the Word was made Flesh.

R. And dwelt among us.

V. Hail Mary, full of grace, the Lord is with thee. Blessed art thou among women, and blessed is the fruit of thy womb, Jesus.

R. Holy Mary, mother of God, pray for us sinners, now, and at the hour of our death. Amen.

V. Pray for us, O holy Mother of God.

R. That we may be made worthy of the promises of Christ.

Let us pray: Pour forth, we beseech thee, O Lord, thy grace into our hearts, that we to whom the Incarnation of Christ thy Son was made known by the message of an angel, may by his Passion and Cross be brought to the glory of his Resurrection. Through the same Christ Our Lord.

R. Amen

Prayer to Our Lady of the Miraculous Medal

VIRGIN Mother of God, Mary Immaculate, we unite ourselves to you under your title of Our Lady of the Miraculous Medal.

May this medal be for each one of us a sure sign of your motherly affection for us and a constant reminder of our filial duties toward you.

While wearing it, may we be blessed by your loving protection and preserved in the grace of your Son.

Most powerful Virgin, Mother of our Savior, keep us close to you every moment of our lives so that like you, we may live and act according to the teaching and example of your Son.

Obtain for us, your children, the grace of a happy death so that in union with you, we may enjoy the happiness of heaven forever.

Amen.

O Mary, conceived without sin, pray for us who have recourse to you.

Prayers by Catholic Saints

You are Christ
(By St. Augustine)

YOU are Christ, my Holy Father, my Tender God, my Great King, my Good Shepherd, my Only Master, my Best Helper, my Most Beautiful and my Beloved, my Living Bread, my Priest Forever, my Leader to my Country, my True Light, my Holy Sweetness, my Straight Way, my Excellent Wisdom, my Pure Simplicity, my Peaceful Harmony, my Entire Protection, my Good Portion, my Everlasting Salvation.

Christ Jesus, Sweet Lord, why have I ever loved, why in my whole life have I ever desired anything except you, Jesus my God? Where was I when I was not in spirit with you? Now, from this time forth, do you, all my desires, grow hot, and flow out upon the Lord Jesus: run . . . you have been tardy until now; hasten where you are going; seek Whom you are seeking. O, Jesus may he who loves you not be an anathema; may he who loves you not be filled with bitterness.

O, Sweet Jesus, may every good feeling that is fitted for your praise, love you, delight in you, adore you! God of my heart, and my Portion, Christ Jesus, may my heart faint away in spirit, and may you be my Life within me! May the live coal of your Love grow hot within my spirit and break forth into a perfect fire; may it burn incessantly on the altar of my heart; may it glow in my innermost being; may it blaze in hidden recesses of my soul; and in the days of my consummation may I be found consummated with you! Amen.

Praise to Mary the Mother of Jesus
(By St. Francis of Assisi)

HAIL, holy Lady, most holy Queen,
Mary, Mother of God, ever Virgin.

You were chosen by the Most High Father in heaven,
consecrated by him, with his most Holy Beloved Son and
the Holy Spirit, the Comforter.

On you descended, and still remains, all the fullness of
grace and every good.

Hail, his Palace.
Hail his Tabernacle.
Hail his Robe.
Hail his Handmaid.

Hail, his Mother and Hail, all holy Virtues, who, by grace
and inspiration of the Holy Spirit, are poured into the hearts
of the faithful so that from their faithless state, they may be
made faithful servants of God through you. Amen.

Canticle of Brother Sun

(By St. Francis of Assisi)

Most high, all powerful, all good Lord!
All praise is yours, all glory, all honor, and all blessing.
To you, alone, Most High, do they belong.
No mortal lips are worthy to pronounce your name.

Be praised, my Lord, through all your creatures,
especially through my lord Brother Sun,
who brings the day; and you give light through him.
And he is beautiful and radiant in all his splendor!
Of you, Most High, he bears the likeness.
Be praised, my Lord, through Sister Moon and the stars;
in the heavens you have made them bright, precious and
beautiful.
Be praised, my Lord, through Brothers Wind and Air,
and clouds and storms, and all the weather,
through which you give your creatures sustenance.
Be praised, My Lord, through Sister Water;
she is very useful, and humble, and precious, and pure.
Be praised, my Lord, through Brother Fire,
through whom you brighten the night.
He is beautiful and cheerful, and powerful and strong.
Be praised, my Lord, through our sister Mother Earth,
who feeds us and rules us,
and produces various fruits with colored flowers and herbs.

Be praised, my Lord, through those who forgive for love of
you;
through those who endure sickness and trial.
Happy those who endure in peace,

for by you, Most High, they will be crowned.
Be praised, my Lord, through our Sister Bodily Death,
from whose embrace no living person can escape.
Woe to those who die in mortal sin!
Happy those she finds doing your most holy will.
The second death can do no harm to them.
Praise and bless my Lord, and give thanks,
and serve him with great humility.
Amen.

Short Act of Perfect Love
(By St. Alphonsus de Liguori)

MY GOD, I love you above all things, and in all things, with my whole soul, because you are worthy of all love!

Sunday Prayer Before Mass

(By St. Ambrose of Milan)

Lord Jesus Christ,

I approach your banquet table in fear and trembling,
for I am a sinner and dare not rely on my own worth
but only on your goodness and mercy.
I am defiled by many sins in body and soul
and by my unguarded thoughts and words.
Gracious God of majesty and awe,
I seek your protection,
I look for your healing.
Poor troubled sinner that I am,
I appeal to you, the fountain of all mercy.
I cannot bear your judgment,
but I trust in your salvation.
Lord, I show my wounds to you
and uncover my shame before you.
I know my sins are many and great
and they fill me with fear,
but I hope in your mercies,
for they cannot be numbered.
Lord Jesus Christ, eternal king,
divine and human,
crucified for humanity,
look upon me with mercy and hear my prayer,
for I trust in you…
Have mercy on me,
full of sorrow and sin, for the depth of your compassion
never ends.
Praise to you, saving sacrifice,
offered on the wood of the cross for me and for all.

Praise to the noble and precious blood
flowing from the wounds of my crucified Lord,
Jesus Christ and washing away the sins of the whole world.
Remember, Lord, your creatures,
whom you have redeemed with your blood.
I repent of my sins
and I long to put right what I have done.
Merciful Lord, take away all my offences and sins;
purify me in body and soul,
and make me worthy to taste the holy of holies.
May your body and blood, which I intend to receive,
although I am unworthy,
be for me the remission of my sins,
the washing away of my guilt,
the end of my evil thoughts
and the rebirth of my better instincts.
May it spur me on to works pleasing to you and be
profitable to my health in body and soul and a firm defense
against the wiles of my enemies. Amen.

O Lord My God

(By St. Anselm)

O Lord my God,
teach my heart this day
where and how to find you.

You have made me and remade me,
and you have bestowed on me
all the good things I possess,
and still I do not know you.
I have not yet done
that for which I was made.

Teach me to seek you,
for I cannot seek you
unless you teach me,
or find you
unless you show yourself to me.

Let me seek you in my desire;
let me desire you in my seeking.
Let me find you by loving you;
let me love you when I find you.

Amen.

Marian Prayer
(By St. Athanasius)

IT is becoming for you, O Mary,
to be mindful of us,
as you stand near him
who bestowed upon you all graces,
for you are the Mother of God and our queen.
Come to our aid for the sake of the king,
the Lord God and master who was born of you.
For this reason you are called "full of grace."
Be mindful of us, most holy Virgin,
and bestow on us gifts
from the riches of your graces,
O Virgin full of grace.
Amen.

For Seekers of Faith
(By St. Benedict)

GRACIOUS and holy Father,
give us the wisdom to discover you,
the intelligence to understand you,
the diligence to seek after you,
the patience to wait for you,
eyes to behold you,
a heart to meditate upon you,
and a life to proclaim you,
through the power of the spirit of Jesus, our Lord.
Amen.

A Student's Prayer

(By St. Thomas Aquinas)

CREATOR of all things,
true source of light and wisdom,
origin of all being,
graciously let a ray of your light
penetrate the darkness of my understanding.

Take from me the double darkness in which I have been born,
an obscurity of sin and of ignorance.

Give me a keen understanding,
a retentive memory,
and the ability to grasp things correctly and fundamentally.

Grant me the talent of being exact in my explanations
and the ability to express myself with thoroughness and charm.

Point out the beginning,
direct the progress,
and help the completion.
I ask this through Jesus Christ our Lord.

Amen.

Morning Prayers

(Upon awaking)

IN THE name of the Father, and of the Son, and of the Holy Spirit. Amen.

I rise in the name of Our Lord Jesus Christ, who redeemed me by his precious blood. Bless, guide, and protect me from all evil, O Lord! Help me to do good and lead me to eternal life. Amen.

(After dressing)

My Lord and my God! I prostrate myself before the throne of your divine majesty, and give you infinite thanks, O Lord, that I have passed this night safely and have not died in my sins, but was preserved by your bounty for your further service.

I offer up to you all that I will do and suffer today, and unite it with the prayers, labors, and sufferings of Our Lord Jesus Christ and of his blessed mother Mary. Amen.

OFFERING

TAKE, O Lord, and receive all my liberty, my memory, my understanding, and my whole will. You have given me all that I am and all that I possess; I surrender it all to you that you may dispose of it according to your will. Give me only your love and your grace; with these I will be rich enough, and will have nothing more to desire. Amen.

Acts of Faith, Hope, and Charity

My LORD and God! I most firmly believe all that you have revealed and all that your holy Church believes and teaches, because you, who are infallible Truth, have revealed these truths and commanded that they be believed.

My Lord and God! Because you are almighty, infinitely good and merciful, I hope that by the merits of the passion and death of Jesus Christ, our Savior, you will grant me eternal life, which you have promised to all who do the works of a good Christian, as I intend to do by your help.

My Lord and God! Because you are the highest and most perfect good, I love you with my whole heart, and above all things; and rather than offend you, I am ready to lose everything else; and for the sake of your love, I love and desire to love my neighbor as myself.

Amen.

Prayer of Consecration to the Blessed Virgin Mary

MY QUEEN, my Mother! I give myself entirely to you; and to show my devotion to you I consecrate to you this day my eyes, my ears, my mouth, my heart, my whole being, without reserve. Since, good Mother, I am yours, keep and guard me as your property and possession.

Amen.

Prayer to One's Guardian Angel

ANGEL of God, my guardian dear,
To whom God's love commits me here,
Ever this day be at my side,
To light and guard, to rule and guide! Amen.

Evening Prayers

ETERNAL and merciful God! I adore you and give you thanks for all the graces and benefits which you have conferred upon me during my whole life, and particularly during this day. May the saints and the elect praise and thank you for me.

Enlighten me now through your Holy Spirit, and let me know whether and how I have offended you today in thought, word, deed, and omission of duty.

Examine your conscience.

An Act of Contrition

O MY God! I am deeply sorry for all my sins, for those I committed today, and for those of my whole life, because I offended your supreme and most loving goodness. Pardon me for the sake of Jesus, your Son, who shed his most precious blood on the cross for our sins. With the help of your grace, I firmly resolve to amend my life, and would rather die than offend you again by a mortal sin. Amen.

Petition for Protection

Protect me and mine and all men during this night and through the intercession of the blessed Virgin Mary, preserve us from all dangers of body and soul. Keep away from us sickness, fire, and calamities of every kind. Protect us against the assaults of the wicked and of Satan. Into your hands I commend my body and soul; let me rest in your most holy wounds.

O Lord, visit this household and repel from it all the snares of the enemy; let your holy angels dwell here to preserve us in peace, and may your blessings remain with us forever. We ask this through Christ our Lord. Amen.

To the Sacred Heart of Jesus
(Prayer of St Alphonsus de Liguori)

ADORABLE heart of my Jesus, heart created expressly for the love of men! Until now I have shown you only ingratitude. Pardon me, O my Jesus! Heart of my Jesus, abyss of love and of mercy, how is it possible that I do not die of sorrow when I reflect on your goodness to me and my ingratitude to you? You, my Creator, after having created me, have given your blood and your life for me; and, not content with this, you have invented a means of offering yourself up every day for me in the Holy Eucharist, exposing yourself to a thousand insults and outrages. O Jesus, fill my heart with a great contrition for my sins, and give me a lively love for you. Through your tears and your blood give me the grace of perseverance in your fervent love until I breathe my last sigh. Amen.

To St. Joseph

SAINT Joseph, father and guardian of virgins, to whose faithful care Christ Jesus, innocence itself, and Mary, the virgin of virgins, were committed, I pray and beseech of you by these dear pledges, Jesus and Mary, to save me from all uncleanness, and to keep my mind untainted, my heart pure, and my body chaste. Help me always to serve Jesus and Mary in perfect chastity all the days of my life. Amen.

Before Retiring
(Prayer of St. Alphonsus de Liguori)

My LORD and God Jesus Christ! I adore you and give you thanks for all the graces which you have granted me today. I offer up to you my rest and every moment of this night, and implore you to preserve me from all sin. Therefore I place myself into the wound of your sacred side, and beneath the protecting mantle of my mother Mary. May your holy angels assist me and watch over my sleeping, and may your holy blessing remain with me. Amen.

Invocation

JESUS, Mary, and Joseph, I give you my heart and my soul.
Jesus, Mary, and Joseph, assist me in my last agony.
Jesus, Mary, and Joseph, may I breathe forth my soul in peace with you. Amen.

Prayers at Holy Mass

Preparatory Prayer

ALMIGHTY and eternal God! I appear in your presence to assist at the most holy sacrifice of the body and blood of Jesus Christ, your Son, my Redeemer, and to offer it up jointly with the priest and the faithful here present, in grateful remembrance of his passion and death, for the promotion of your glory, and for my salvation. Together with all the holy Masses that are celebrated throughout the world, I offer up this sacrifice for the following intentions: To adore you, O my God, as you deserve to be adored; to give you thanks for the innumerable benefits which I owe to your bounty; to make reparation for the many offenses I have committed; to appease your just anger, and to invoke your infinite mercy for me, for your holy Church, for the whole world, and for the souls in purgatory. Amen.

At the Beginning of Mass

O HEAVENLY Father! Hear the prayer of your holy
Church invoking your divine majesty in the name of Our
Lord Jesus Christ to come to the aid of your children in all
their needs. Turn not from us your gracious eyes, but
deliver us from all evil, so that we may live to please you,
die in your love, and enter the kingdom of glory. Amen.

At the Creed

Say the Apostles' Creed:

I believe in God, the Father Almighty, Creator of heaven and earth, and in Jesus Christ, his only Son, our Lord, who was conceived by the Holy Spirit, born of the Virgin Mary, suffered under Pontius Pilate, was crucified, died and was buried; he descended into hell; on the third day he rose again from the dead; he ascended into heaven, and is seated at the right hand of God the Father almighty; from there he will come to judge the living and the dead. I believe in the Holy Spirit, the holy Catholic Church, the communion of saints, the forgiveness of sins, the resurrection of the body, and life everlasting.
Amen.

At the Offertory

ALMIGHTY and eternal God! Look graciously on the forms of bread and wine offered up to you on the altar by the priest, imploring you to bless and sanctify them for the eucharistic sacrifice of the New Law. With this sacrifice, O my God, I offer up to you my heart with all its affections, desires, and inclinations. Sanctify my thoughts, words, and deeds, that they may become a sacrifice acceptable and pleasing to you. Amen.

At the Sanctus

HOLY, holy, holy Lord God of hosts.
Heaven and earth are full of your glory.
Hosanna in the highest.
Blessed is he who comes in the name of the Lord.
Hosanna in the highest.

At the Elevation

MY Lord and my God!

At the Our Father

OUR Father who art in heaven,
hallowed be thy name.
Thy kingdom come.
Thy will be done
on earth as it is in heaven.
Give us this day our daily bread,
and forgive us our trespasses,
as we forgive those who trespass against us,
and lead us not into temptation,
but deliver us from evil.

At the Agnus Dei

Lamb of God, who takes away the sins of the world, have mercy on us.
Lamb of God, who takes away the sins of the world, have mercy on us.
Lamb of God, who takes away the sins of the world, grant us peace.

At Communion

LORD, I am not worthy that you should enter under my roof, but only say the word and my soul shall be healed.

Spiritual Communion

O JESUS, I firmly believe that you are truly present in the Blessed Sacrament. I see you full of love, willing to pardon us, anxious to be united with us. I wish most earnestly to respond to your desire and love. I detest all the sins by which I have ever displeased you. Pardon me, O Lord! I desire to receive you into my heart, and since I now cannot receive you sacramentally, come at least spiritually to me.

I embrace you, I unite myself with you as if you were really present in my heart. With all my love I cling to you. Preserve me from sin, that I may never be separated from you, but remain united with you forever. Amen.

Prayers after Mass

Salve Regina

Hail, holy queen, Mother of mercy, our life, our sweetness, and our hope! To thee do we cry, poor banished children of Eve; to thee do we send up our sighs, mourning and weeping in this vale of tears. Turn then, most gracious advocate, thine eyes of mercy toward us, and after this our exile show unto us the blessed fruit of thy womb, Jesus. O clement, O loving, O sweet Virgin Mary!

V. Pray for us, O holy Mother of God.

R. That we may be made worthy of the promises of Christ.

Let Us Pray.

O God, our refuge and our strength! Look down with favor upon thy people crying to thee; and through the intercession of the glorious and immaculate Virgin Mary, Mother of God, of her spouse, blessed Joseph, of thy holy apostles Peter and Paul, and all thy saints, mercifully and graciously hear the prayers which we pour forth to thee for the conversion of sinners and for the liberty and exaltation of holy mother Church. Through Christ our Lord. Amen.

Prayer to Saint Michael

St. Michael the archangel, defend us in battle; be our protection against the malice and snares of the devil. Command him, O God, we humbly beseech thee, and do thou, O prince of the heavenly hosts, by the divine power, cast into hell Satan and the other evil spirits who roam through the world seeking the ruin of souls. Amen.

Prayers for Confession

Before Confession

MERCIFUL God! I thank you for the many and great graces you have bestowed on me during my life. I wish that I had never been ungrateful to you, that I had never offended you. But I have sinned exceedingly and often, and have done so again since my last confession. Therefore I come to you, imploring you in profoundest humility to give me your light and your grace, that I may know and acknowledge all my sins, faults, and transgressions, be truly sorry for them, sincerely confess them, do penance, and amend my life, for your greater glory and for the salvation of my soul.

Examine your conscience.

SUPREME God and Lord! A poor sinner, I cast myself at the throne of your divine majesty, and contritely confess that I have sinned in thought, word, and deed, and through the omission of my duties. I am heartily sorry that I was ungrateful to you and have deserved to be punished in this life and in the life to come. Above all I am sorry because by my sins I have offended you, my supreme and infinite God, who are worthy to be loved and honored above all else for your supreme goodness and mercy. I detest and abhor my sins above all other evils, and wish I had never committed them. Humbly I implore your pardon, and confidently hope to obtain it through the merits of the blood of Jesus Christ shed for us poor sinners, and through those of the Blessed Virgin Mary and of all the saints.

I firmly resolve to amend my life, to avoid all occasions of sin, to use the means for conquering my passions, and to practice virtue by ordering my life according to your divine will and pleasure, and would rather die than offend you again, my God and Lord. I am now ready to make reparation to your divine justice for all the offenses of which I have been guilty against you, as far as is in my power. Therefore I will confess my sins sincerely, contritely, fully, and perform the penance imposed upon me. Amen.

Before Entering the Confessional

May the Lord be in my heart and on my lips, that I may worthily and competently confess my sins. Amen.

After Confession

O GOD of infinite mercy! I give you thanks and praise you for having admitted me to the confession of my sins and for having, through your minister, granted me absolution for them. I implore you by the merits of Jesus Christ your Son, of Mary, his most blessed mother, and of all the saints, to accept my confession, and in your infinite mercy to condone and amend all the defects and faults I committed in making it, and to ratify in heaven the absolution I received on earth.

O my Jesus! How blind I was in not knowing you and preferring transitory beauty and earthly attractions to your grace and love, thereby offending you! Now I acknowledge my fault, and am convinced that it is my duty and privilege to love you above all things. Too late I have learned it, but I shall zealously strive to make reparation for my past neglect. Therefore I renounce the pleasures, vanities, and joys of this deceitful world, and abhor sin and all that leads to it. In the future nothing shall ever part me from your love. From this moment on I am resolved nevermore to offend you. Confirm, O Jesus, my resolution, and with your almighty power strengthen my frailty. Seal my purpose of amendment with the bestowal of your grace, and preserve me in your grace and love to the end.

Amen.

Prayers for Holy Communion

BEFORE COMMUNION

An Act of Faith

MY LORD and Savior Jesus Christ! I firmly believe that you are really present in the Blessed Sacrament. I believe it contains your body and blood, your soul and divinity. I acknowledge these truths and believe these wonders. I adore your power which has wrought them and I praise your infinite goodness which has prepared them for me. "I will praise you, my God, with my whole heart, and will recount all your admirable works; I will rejoice in you, and bless your holy name" (Ps. 9:1-2). In this faith, and with this acknowledgment, I presume to approach this adorable banquet, wherein you bestow on me the divine food of your body and blood to nourish my soul. Grant, O Jesus, that I may approach you with the sense of reverence and humility that your divine majesty deserves. Who am I, O God, that you should work such wonders for my sake? Grant, O Lord, that I may not be altogether unworthy of them, and that I may now receive you with a pure heart, a clean conscience, and a sincere and lively faith. Pardon my sins, which have made me most unworthy to approach you. I detest them from the bottom of my heart, because they are displeasing to you, my God. I renounce them forever, and promise to be faithful to you. Amen.

An Act of Hope

IN you, sweet Jesus, I place all my hope, because you alone are my salvation, my strength, my refuge, and the foundation of all my happiness. Were it not for the confidence I place in your merits, and in the precious blood you shed for my redemption, I would not presume to partake of this banquet. Encouraged, therefore, by your goodness, I come to you as one sick to his physician, as a condemned criminal to his powerful intercessor. Heal me as my physician and, as my powerful advocate, deliver me from the sentence of sin and death. It is in your mercy that I put all my trust. O Jesus, have pity on me and save me, for you forsake none who place their hope in you. Amen.

An Act of Love

O DIVINE Redeemer, how strong was the force of your love, that, being about to depart from this world to your eternal Father, you provided for us this divine banquet, enriched with all heavenly sweetness! It was through an excess of your love that you have left us your body and blood for the food and nourishment of our souls so that as you united yourself to our humanity, we might be partakers of your divinity. I desire to love you, my Jesus, who are my only comfort in this place of banishment, the only hope of my infirm soul, my happiness above all that I might enjoy in this life. I love you, my God, with all my whole heart, soul, mind and strength. I wish that, as every moment is an increase of my life, so it may also be of my love toward you. I desire, with all the affections and powers of my soul, that, as the inmost thanks are due to you, so they may be returned to you by all the faithful, for this divine food, which is our refreshment, support, strength, armor, and defense in all our miseries; and that my love may never cease, inflame my heart with the fire of heaven, that it may continue burning until I may at last be transformed into you. Come, O Lord, hasten to release me from the bonds of sin, and prepare me for the blessing you are now about to bestow on me. Amen.

An Act of Humility

O IMMENSE, almighty, and incomprehensible God, who am I, that you should become my food and take your dwelling within my soul? The thought of your greatness and my unworthiness penetrates me with awe and confusion. I declare that I am in a miserable state and admire that infinite goodness which prompts you to visit the lowest and basest of your creatures. Receive me, your unworthy servant, into the compassionate arms of your mercy. Cast all my sins out of your sight and, with the tenderness of a loving father, extend your arms to receive me. Let me experience the truth of your prophet's words, "A sacrifice to God is an afflicted spirit; a contrite and humble heart, O God, you will not spurn" (Ps. 51:17). Amen.

IMMEDIATELY BEFORE COMMUNION

LORD, I am not worthy that you should enter under my roof, but only say the word, and my soul shall be healed.

AFTER COMMUNION

An Act of Thanksgiving

O JESUS, my God and Savior! I thank you for having, out of your pure mercy, without any desert of mine, been pleased to feed my soul with your own most sacred body and blood. May I sooner forget myself than to be ever unmindful of this great favor. Although I have previously been ungrateful, with the help of your grace I shall be so no more. But what return can I make you, being of myself insolvent, indigent, and miserable? The sacrifice of all that I am or have is not worthy to be presented to you; but, behold I offer you yourself, and consider all my debts as abundantly discharged. May your infinite mercy be forever exalted for having given me such an excellent means of repaying you to the full. O that I could ever remember you, think of you, ever love you alone! Imprint the memory of what you did for me so deeply in my heart, that I may spend my whole life in thanking you for all your benefits, but especially for this banquet of your love. Amen.

An Act of Adoration

UNDER the sacred veil of your eucharistic presence, where your love of man conceals the splendor of your majesty, I most humbly adore you, O almighty God! The grandeur of the heavens is as nothing in your sight; they shall perish, but you shall remain forever. The earth you have placed in your hand. The ocean is before you but as a drop of water. All nature bows and trembles in your presence. How, then, shall I extol you, immortal King of glory? What homage can I give in proportion to your greatness? You are the perfect image of your Father's substance. You are the splendor of his glory. You are his almighty Word, supporting all things. He has seated you at his right hand. Your throne, O God, is forever and ever; a scepter of justice is the scepter of your reign. I bow before your sacred Majesty. I acknowledge with the sincerest gratitude that you are my redeemer, my creator, the supreme arbiter of my eternal destiny. I desire to humble myself as profoundly for your sake as you are humbled for my love in the center of my soul, and to consecrate to the glory of your name the whole extent of my being. Amen.

An Act of Oblation

O MY Savior! What pledge can I give as a token of the gratitude I owe you? I have nothing worthy of you, and if I had, I have nothing but what is yours. But such is your goodness that you are content to accept from us what is already yours. I offer to you my body and soul, which are both now sanctified by the honor of your divine presence. I consecrate them to you forever, since you have chosen them for your temple. May my body be continually employed in your service, and nevermore become an instrument of sin. May my soul know you, love you and be evermore faithful to you. Since I am now resolved to serve you with body and soul, I will carefully correct their evil inclinations. I will master myself, renounce my illicit pleasures, delights, passions, anger, self-love, pride, will, and whatever may offend you. Amen.

Offering and Petition

ALMIGHTY God, I offer you this holy Communion in union with the superabundant merits of Jesus Christ, your beloved Son, and the infinite love of his adorable heart; in union with the Blessed Virgin and the ardent love of her immaculate heart; in union with all the happy souls who enjoy your glorious vision in heaven, and with all the just on earth. O my God and Savior, Jesus Christ, present in me in the eucharistic species; fill me with that lively faith, profound humility, tender confidence, pure conscience, and ardent love, with which so many happy souls are inflamed in partaking of this sacred banquet, and supply by your mercy all my deficiencies. I offer my communion to give you the honor and glory which are due to your infinite majesty; to satisfy your justice, which I have provoked by my sins; to thank you for the innumerable benefits which I have received from your bounty; and to obtain from your infinite mercy the graces necessary for me; particularly the grace to subdue my predominant passion and to acquire the virtue in which I am most deficient; but especially the grace of a happy death.

I likewise offer my communion, O merciful Father, in memory of the passion and death of your dear Son, my divine Redeemer, to love him with more ardor and perfection; to participate in the merits of his labors and sufferings; to acquire his spirit; to imitate his virtues; to model my life on his, and to make his adorable Heart a public reparation for all the sacrilegious communions, irreverences, and profanations which are committed against him in this sacrament of his love. I offer it to thank you, O God, for all the graces you have bestowed on mankind, particularly for all those you have conferred on your blessed Mother, on all the angels and saints, especially on my guardian angel, and on my holy patron. I offer it for the Catholic Church, for the conversion of unbelievers, those who do not accept the truth, our separated brethren, and all those who are in the unhappy state of sin. I also pray for the needs of my relatives, friends, benefactors, and enemies; for the perseverance of the just, the comfort of the afflicted, and the deliverance of the souls in purgatory; in a word, I pray for all those for whom I am bound to pray. Amen.

Anima Christi

SOUL of Christ, sanctify me!
Body of Christ, save me!
Blood of Christ, inebriate me!
Water from the side of Christ, wash me!
Passion of Christ, strengthen me!
O good Jesus, hear me!
Within thy wounds, hide me!
Permit me not to be separated from thee!
From the malicious enemy defend me!
In the hour of my death call me!
And bid me come to thee,
That, with thy saints, I may praise thee
For ever and ever. Amen.

Prayer to Jesus Crucified

LOOK down upon me, good and gentle Jesus, humbly kneeling before you. With tremendous fervor I pray and ask you to instill in me genuine convictions of faith, hope, and love, true sorrow for my sins, and a firm purpose of amendment. While I contemplate your five wounds with great love and tender compassion, I call to mind the words which the prophet David put on your lips: "They pierced my hands and my feet; I can count all my bones" (Ps. 22:16-17).

Visit to the Blessed Sacrament

(By St. Alphonsus de Liguori)

LORD Jesus Christ, through the love which you have for man, you have chosen to remain with us day and night in this sacrament, full of mercy and love, expecting, inviting, and receiving all who come to visit you. I believe that you are present in the Sacrament of the Altar. From the abyss of my nothingness I adore you, and I thank you for all the favors which you have bestowed upon me, particularly for having given me yourself in this sacrament, for having given me your most holy mother Mary for my advocate, and for having called me to visit you in this church.

I salute your most loving heart in thanksgiving for this great gift and in compensation for all the injuries you have received from your enemies in this sacrament. I wish by this visit to adore you in all places in which you are least honored and most abandoned in this holy sacrament. My Jesus, I love you with my whole heart. I am sorry for having previously offended your infinite goodness. I resolve, with the aid of your grace, to never offend you again. I consecrate my whole being to you and give you my entire will, all my affections and desires, and all that I have. From this day forward, do with me what you will. I desire only your holy love, the gift of final perseverance, and the perfect accomplishment of your will. I pray for the souls in purgatory, particularly those who were most devoted to the Blessed Sacrament and to the Blessed Virgin Mary, and for all poor sinners. Finally, my dear Savior, I unite all my affections with the affections of your most loving heart, and offer these united affections to your eternal Father, entreating him to accept them in your name. Amen.

An Act of Oblation to the Sacred Heart

DIVINE heart of my Jesus! I adore you with all the powers of my soul, which I consecrate to you forever along with my thoughts, my words, my works, and my whole self. I endeavor to offer you acts of adoration, love, and glory, like those which you offered to your eternal Father. Repair my transgressions, protect my life, and be my refuge and asylum in the hour of death. By your sighs, and by that sea of bitterness in which you were plunged for me throughout your whole mortal life, grant me true contrition for my sins, contempt of earthly things, a burning desire of eternal glory, trust in your infinite merits, and final perseverance in your grace.

Heart of Jesus, all love, I offer you these humble prayers for myself and for all who unite with me in spirit to adore you. In your goodness, hear and answer them. Have mercy especially on the one among us who will end this mortal life soonest. Sweet heart of Jesus, pour into his heart your consolation, receive him in your sacred wound, and cleanse him from all stains in that furnace of love so that the gates of your eternal glory may soon open for him.

Most holy heart of my most loving Jesus! For myself, a poor sinner, and for all who unite with me in adoring you, I resolve to offer you these acts of adoration and these prayers at every moment of my life. I pray for our holy Church, your well-beloved spouse and our true mother, the souls who are following the path of justice, poor sinners, the afflicted, the dying, and all people on the face of the earth. Do not let your blood be shed in vain for them. Be pleased to apply your blood for the relief of the souls in purgatory, and above all, for those who in life were foremost in their devotion to you.

Most loving heart of Mary, which among the hearts of all God's creatures is the purest and the most inflamed with love for Jesus and the most compassionate toward us poor sinners, obtain for us from the heart of Jesus all graces which we ask of you. Mother of mercies, a single beat of your burning heart, offered by you to the heart of Jesus, has power to console us perfectly. Grant us this favor so that the heart of Jesus, through the filial love he has for you, will hear and answer our request. Amen.

DAILY OFFERING

O LORD Jesus Christ! In union with that divine intention, with which you, while on earth, gave praise to God through your most Sacred Heart, and with which you continue to offer to him in the Holy Eucharist until the consummation of the world, in imitation of the most Immaculate Heart of the ever Virgin Mary, I gladly offer you this day all my thoughts, intentions, affections, desires, words, and works. Amen.

Ejaculation

Jesus, meek and humble of heart, make my heart like yours!

The Stations of the Cross

PREPARATORY PRAYER

MOST merciful Jesus! With a contrite heart and penitent spirit I bow down in profound humility before your divine majesty. I adore you as my supreme Lord and master. I believe in you, I hope in you, and I love you above all things. I am heartily sorry for having offended you, my supreme and only good. I resolve to amend my life. Although I am unworthy to obtain mercy, the sight of your0 holy cross, on which you died, inspires me with hope and consolation. Therefore, I will meditate on your sufferings and visit the stations of your passion in company with your sorrowful mother and my guardian angel, with the intention of promoting your glory and making reparation for my sins.
I desire to gain all the indulgences granted for this exercise, for myself and for the suffering souls in purgatory. O merciful Redeemer, who has said, "And I, if I be lifted up from the earth, will draw all things to myself" (John 12:32) draw my heart and my love to you that I may perform this devotion as perfectly as possible, and that I may live and die in union with you. Amen.

Before Every Station

V. We adore you, O Christ, and we praise you,
R. Because by your holy cross, you have redeemed the world.

After Every Station

Our Father

Hail Mary

First Station

JESUS IS CONDEMNED TO DEATH

J ESUS, most innocent, who neither did nor could commit sin, was condemned to death, and, moreover, to the ignominious death of the cross. To remain a friend of Caesar, Pilate delivered him to his enemies. A fearful crime—to condemn innocence to death, and to offend God, in order not to displease men.

Prayer

O INNOCENT Jesus, having sinned I am guilty of eternal death, but you willingly accepted the unjust sentence of death, that I might live. For whom, then, shall I live, if not for you, my Lord? If I wanted to please men, I could not be your servant. I would rather displease men and all the world than not please you, O Jesus.

Second Station

JESUS CARRIES HIS CROSS

ON BEHOLDING the cross, our divine Savior most willingly stretched out his bleeding arms, lovingly embraced it, tenderly kissed it, placed it on his bruised shoulder, and despite his exhaustion, joyfully carried it.

Prayer

O MY Jesus, I cannot be your friend and follower if I refuse to carry the cross. O dearly beloved cross, I embrace you, I kiss you, I rejoice to receive you from the hands of God. Far be it from me to glory in anything save in the cross of my Lord and Redeemer, by which the world shall be crucified to me, and I to the world, that I may belong to God forever.

Third Station

JESUS FALLS THE FIRST TIME

OUR dear Savior was so weakened by the heavy weight of the cross that he fell to the ground. Our sins and misdeeds were the heavy burden which oppressed him; the cross was to him light and sweet, but our sins were galling and insupportable.

Prayer

O MY Jesus! You bore my burden and the heavy weight of my sins. Should I, then, not bear in union with you my easy burden of suffering and accept the sweet yoke of your commandments? Your yoke is sweet and your burden light; I therefore willingly accept it. I will take up your cross and follow you.

Fourth Station

JESUS MEETS HIS AFFLICTED MOTHER

HOW painful and how sad it must have been for Mary, the sorrowful Mother, to behold her beloved son laden with the burden of the cross! What unspeakable pangs her most tender heart experienced! How earnestly she yearned to die instead of Jesus! Implore this sorrowful mother to assist you in the hour of your death.

Prayer

O JESUS, O Mary! I am the cause of the great and manifold pains which pierce your loving hearts. O that my heart would feel and experience at least some of your sufferings! O Mother of Sorrows, let me participate in the sufferings which you and your son endured for me, and let me experience your sorrow, that, afflicted with you, I may enjoy your assistance in the hour of my death.

Fifth Station

SIMON OF CYRENE HELPS JESUS TO CARRY THE CROSS

SIMON of Cyrene was compelled to help Jesus carry his cross, and Jesus accepted his assistance. How willingly he would permit you also to carry the cross! He calls you, but you hear him not; he invites you, but you decline. What a reproach, to bear the cross reluctantly!

Prayer

O JESUS! Whosoever does not take up his cross and follow you is not worthy of you. Behold, I join you in the way of your cross; I will be your assistant, following your footsteps, that I may come to you in eternal life.

Sixth Station

VERONICA WIPES THE FACE OF JESUS

IMPELLED by devotion and compassion, Veronica presents her veil to Jesus to wipe his disfigured face. And Jesus imprints on it his holy countenance; a great recompense for so slight a service. What return do you make to your Savior for his great and manifold benefits?

Prayer

MOST merciful Jesus! What return shall I make for all the benefits you bestowed on me? Behold, I consecrate myself entirely to your service. I offer and consecrate to you my heart; imprint upon it your sacred image so that it will never be effaced by sin again.

Seventh Station

JESUS FALLS THE SECOND TIME

JESUS, suffering under the weight of his cross, again falls to the ground; but his cruel executioners do not permit him to rest a moment. Pushing and striking him, they urge him onward. It is the frequent repetition of our sins which oppresses Jesus. Witnessing this, how can I continue to sin?

Prayer

O JESUS, son of David, have mercy on me! Offer me your helping hand, and aid me that I may not fall again into my former sins. From this very moment I will earnestly strive to reform; nevermore will I sin. O Lord, sole support of the weak, give me your grace and strength so that I may be empowered to carry out this resolution faithfully.

Eighth Station

THE DAUGHTERS OF JERUSALEM WEEP OVER JESUS

THESE devoted women, moved by compassion, weep over the suffering Savior. But he turns to them, saying, "Weep not for me, who am innocent, but weep for yourselves and for your children." You too should weep, for there is nothing more pleasing to Our Lord, and nothing more profitable for yourself, than tears shed from contrition for your sins.

Prayer

O JESUS, who will give my eyes a torrent of tears so that day and night I may weep for my sins? I ask you Lord, who wept tears of blood, to move my heart by your divine grace, so that from my eyes tears may flow abundantly. May I weep everyday over your sufferings, and even more so over my sins, which have caused you to suffer.

Ninth Station

JESUS FALLS THE THIRD TIME

JESUS, arriving exhausted at the foot of Calvary, falls for the third time to the ground. His love for us is not exhausted or diminished. What a fearfully oppressive burden our sins must be to cause Jesus to fall so often! Had he, however, not taken them upon himself, they would have plunged us into the abyss of hell.

Prayer

MOST merciful Jesus! I thank you for not permitting me to continue in sin, and to fall, as I have so often deserved, into the depths of hell. Enkindle in me an earnest desire of amendment. Let me never again relapse, but give me your grace so that I may persevere to the end of my life.

Tenth Station

JESUS IS STRIPPED OF HIS GARMENTS

AFTER arriving on Calvary, our Savior was cruelly despoiled of his garments. How painful must this have been, because they adhered to his wounded and torn body, and with them parts of his bloody skin were removed! All the wounds of Jesus are renewed. He is despoiled of his garments that he might die possessed of nothing. How happy shall I die after laying aside my former self with all evil inclinations and desires!

Prayer

INSPIRE me, O Jesus, to lay aside my former self, and to be renewed according to your will. I will not spare myself, however painful this might be for me. Despoiled of temporal things, of my own will, I desire to die in order to live for you forever.

Eleventh Station

JESUS IS NAILED TO THE CROSS

JESUS, being stripped of his garments, was violently thrown upon the cross, and his hands and feet were most cruelly nailed to the wood. In such excruciating torments he remained silent, because it thus pleased his heavenly Father. He suffered patiently because he suffered for us. How do I act in suffering and affliction? How fretful and impatient, how full of complaints I am!

Prayer

O JESUS, gracious Lamb of God! I renounce for ever my impatience. Crucify, O Lord, my flesh and its concupiscence. Punish me in this world, but spare me in the next! I commit my destiny to you, resigning myself to your holy will. May your will be done in all things.

Twelfth Station

JESUS IS RAISED UPON THE CROSS, AND DIES

BEHOLD Jesus crucified! Behold the wounds he received for the love of you! His whole appearance suggests his love. His arms are extended to embrace you and his heart is open to receive you. O superabundance of love! Jesus, the Son of God dies that we might live and be delivered from everlasting death!

Prayer

O MOST amiable Jesus, who will permit me to die for love of you? I will at least endeavor to die to the world. How can I regard the world and its vanities, when I behold you hanging on the cross, covered with wounds? O Jesus, receive me into your wounded heart; I belong entirely to you. I desire to live and die for you alone.

Thirteenth Station

JESUS IS TAKEN DOWN FROM THE CROSS AND PLACED IN THE ARMS OF HIS MOTHER

J ESUS did not descend from the cross, but remained on it until he died. When he was taken down from it, he, in death as in life, rested on the bosom of his mother. Persevere in your resolutions of reform, and do not part from the cross; he that perseveres to the end shall be saved (Matt. 24:13). Consider, moreover, how pure the heart should be that receives the body and blood of Christ in the adorable Sacrament of the Altar, and resolve to be pure.

Prayer

O LORD Jesus, your lifeless body, mangled and torn, found a worthy resting place on the bosom of your mother. Have I not begged you often to dwell in my heart, full of sin and impurity as it was? Create in me a new heart so that I may worthily receive your most sacred body in holy Communion, and that you may remain in me and I in you for all eternity.

Fourteenth Station

JESUS IS LAID IN THE SEPULCHER

THE body of Jesus is laid in a stranger's tomb. He, who in this world had nowhere to rest his head, would not even have a grave of his own, because he was not of this world. You, who are so attached to the world, despise it from now on so that you may not perish with it.

Prayer

O JESUS, you have set me apart from the world and have created me for heaven; what, then, have I to do with the world? Depart from me, deceitful world, with your vanities! From this moment on I will follow the way of the cross traced out for me by my Redeemer, and journey onward to my heavenly home, there to dwell for ever and ever.

CONCLUSION

ALMIGHTY and eternal God, merciful Father, who gave to the human race your beloved son as an example of humility, obedience, and patience as he bore his cross, graciously grant that we, inflamed by his infinite love, may take up the sweet yoke of his Gospel, together with the mortification of the cross, and follow him as his true disciples so that we may one day rise gloriously with him, and joyfully hear the final sentence, "Come, you blessed of my Father, and possess the kingdom which has been prepared for you from the beginning" (Matt. 25:34). In this kingdom, where your son reigns with you and the Holy Spirit, we hope to reign with him for all eternity. Amen.

Prayer to Our Suffering Redeemer

O MY Lord Jesus Christ, you were pleased to be born among men, to be circumcised, to be rejected and persecuted by the Jews, to be betrayed by the traitor Judas with a kiss, and as a lamb, gentle and innocent, to be bound with cords and dragged before the tribunals of Annas, Caiaphas, Pilate, and Herod. You endured false accusations, were scourged and insulted, spat upon, crowned with thorns, buffeted, struck with a reed, blindfolded, stripped of your garments, nailed to the cross, raised on it between two thieves, given gall and vinegar to drink, and pierced with a lance. By your sufferings, O Lord, and by your holy cross and death, save me from the pains of hell, and be pleased to bring me where you brought the good thief who was crucified with you, who with the Father and the Holy Spirit, lives and reigns one God, forever and ever. Amen.

Prayer to the Blessed Virgin Mary

(By St. Alphonsus de Liguori)

Most holy and immaculate virgin, O my mother and mother of my Lord, the queen of the world, the advocate, hope, and refuge of sinners! I, the most wretched among them, come now to you. I venerate you, great queen, and give you thanks for the many favors you have bestowed on me in the past. Most of all, I thank you for having saved me from hell, which I so often deserved. I love you, lady most worthy of love, and I promise to serve you in the future and to win others to your love. In you I put all my trust and my hope of salvation. Receive me as your servant, and cover me with the mantle of your protection, O mother of mercy! Since your intercession is so powerful with God, deliver me from all temptations, or at least always obtain for me the grace to overcome them. Pray that I may be given a true love of Jesus Christ and the grace of a happy death. O my mother, by your love for God, I ask you to be my helper from now on, but above all at the last moment of my life. Do not leave me until I am safely in heaven. Amen.

Prayer for All Things Necessary for Salvation

O MY God, I believe in you; strengthen my faith. All my hopes are in you; secure them. I love you with my whole heart; teach me to love you more and more. I am sorry that I have offended you; increase my sorrow. I adore you as my first beginning; I aspire after you as my last end. I give you thanks as my constant benefactor; I call upon you as my sovereign protector. Be pleased, O my God, to conduct me by your wisdom, to restrain me by your justice, to comfort me by your mercy, to defend me by your power. To you I desire to consecrate all my thoughts, my actions, and my sufferings, that I from now on I may think of you, speak of you, and refer all my actions to your greater glory, and suffer willingly whatever you shall appoint. O Lord, I desire that in all things your will be done, because it is your will, and I desire that all things be done in the manner that you will them. I beg of you to enlighten my understanding, to inflame my will, to purify my body, and to sanctify my soul. Give me strength, O my God, to expiate my offenses, to overcome my temptations, to subdue my passions, and to acquire the virtues proper for my state. Fill my heart with tender affection for your goodness, hatred of my faults, love for my neighbor, and contempt for the world. Let me always be submissive to my superiors, kind and courteous to my inferiors, faithful to my friends, and charitable to my enemies. Assist me to overcome sensuality by mortification, avarice by almsdeeds, anger by meekness, and tepidity by zeal. O my God, make me prudent in my undertakings, courageous in dangers, patient in affliction, and humble in prosperity. Grant that I may be ever attentive at my prayers, temperate at my meals, diligent in my employments, and constant in my resolutions. Let my conscience be ever upright and pure, my exterior modest, my conversation edifying, my conduct upright. Assist me that I may continually strive to overcome the evil inclinations of my nature, cooperate with your grace, keep your commandments, and work out my salvation. Help me to realize, O my God, the nothingness of this world, the greatness of heaven, the shortness of time, and the length of eternity. Grant that I may be prepared for death, fear your judgments, escape hell and in the end obtain heaven.

All that I have asked for myself I confidently ask for others; for my family, my relations, my benefactors, my friends, and also for my enemies. I ask it for the whole Church, for all the orders of which it is composed; more especially for our Holy Father, the Pope, for our bishop, for our pastors, and for all who are in authority; also for all those for whom I should pray. Give them, O Lord, all that is conducive to your glory and necessary for their salvation. Strengthen the just in virtue, convert sinners, enlighten unbelievers, those who reject the truth, and our separated brethren; console the afflicted, give to the faithful departed rest and eternal life; that together we may praise, love, and bless you for all eternity. Amen.

Litanies

Litany of the Most Holy Name of Jesus

LORD, have mercy.
Lord, have mercy.
Christ, have mercy.
Christ, have mercy.
Lord, have mercy.
Lord, have mercy.
Jesus, hear us.
Jesus, graciously hear us.
God the Father of heaven, **have mercy on us.**
God the Son, Redeemer of the world,
God the Holy Spirit,
Holy Trinity, one God,
Jesus, Son of the living God,
Jesus, splendor of the Father,
Jesus, brightness of eternal light,
Jesus, king of glory,
Jesus, Sun of Justice,
Jesus, Son of the Virgin Mary,
Jesus most amiable,
Jesus most admirable,
Jesus, mighty God,
Jesus, Father of the world to come,
Jesus, Angel of great council,
Jesus most powerful,
Jesus most patient,
Jesus most obedient,
Jesus meek and humble of heart,
Jesus, lover of chastity,
Jesus, lover of us,
Jesus, God of peace,
Jesus, author of life,

Jesus, model of all virtues,
Jesus, zealous lover of souls,
Jesus, our God,
Jesus, our refuge,
Jesus, father of the poor,
Jesus, treasure of the faithful,
Jesus, good shepherd,
Jesus, true light,
Jesus, eternal wisdom,
Jesus, infinite goodness,
Jesus, our way and our life,
Jesus, joy of angels,
Jesus, king of patriarchs,
Jesus, master of the apostles,
Jesus, teacher of the evangelists,
Jesus, strength of martyrs,
Jesus, light of confessors,
Jesus, purity of virgins,
Jesus, crown of all saints,
Be merciful, *spare us, O Jesus.*
Be merciful, *graciously hear us, O Jesus.*
From all evil, ***deliver us, O Jesus.***
From all sin,
From your wrath,
From the snares of the devil,
From the spirit of fornication,
From eternal death,
From neglect of your inspirations,
By the mystery of your holy incarnation,
By your nativity,
By your infancy,
By your most divine life,
By your labors,
By your agony and passion,

By your cross and dereliction,
By your sufferings,
By your death and burial,
By your Resurrection,
By your Ascension,
By your joys,
By your glory,

Lamb of God, who takes away the sins of the world, *spare us, O Jesus.*
Lamb of God, who takes away the sins of the world, *graciously hear us, O Jesus.*
Lamb of God, who takes away the sins of the world, *have mercy on us, O Jesus.*
Jesus, hear us.
Jesus, graciously hear us.

Let us pray

O LORD Jesus Christ, you have said: Ask, and you shall receive, seek and you shall find, knock and it shall be opened to you; grant, we beseech you, to us who ask the gift of your most divine love, that we may ever love you with our whole heart and with all our words and deeds, and may never cease from praising you. Make us, O Lord, to have a perpetual fear and love of your holy name, for you never fail to help and govern those whom you bring up in your steadfast fear and love: who lives and reigns forever and ever. Amen.

Litany of the Sacred Heart of Jesus

LORD, have mercy.
Lord, have mercy.
Christ, have mercy.
Christ, have mercy.
Lord, have mercy.
Lord, have mercy.
Christ, hear us.
Christ, graciously hear us.
God, the Father of heaven, *have mercy on us.*
God the Son, Redeemer of the world,
God the Holy Spirit,
Holy Trinity, one God,
Heart of Jesus, Son of the eternal Father,
Heart of Jesus, formed by the Holy Spirit in the womb of the Virgin Mary,
Heart of Jesus, substantially united to the Word of God,
Heart of Jesus, of infinite majesty,
Heart of Jesus, sacred temple of God,
Heart of Jesus, tabernacle of the Most High,
Heart of Jesus, house of God and gate of heaven,
Heart of Jesus, burning furnace of charity,
Heart of Jesus, abode of justice and love,
Heart of Jesus, full of goodness and love,
Heart of Jesus, wellspring of all virtues,
Heart of Jesus, most worthy of all praise,
Heart of Jesus, king and center of all hearts,
Heart of Jesus, in whom are all the treasures of wisdom and knowledge,
Heart of Jesus, in whom dwells the fullness of divinity,
Heart of Jesus, in whom the Father was well pleased,

Heart of Jesus, of whose fullness we have all received,
Heart of Jesus, desire of the everlasting hills,
Heart of Jesus, patient and most merciful,
Heart of Jesus, enriching all who invoke you,
Heart of Jesus, fountain of life and holiness,
Heart of Jesus, propitiation for our sins,
Heart of Jesus, overwhelmed with insults,
Heart of Jesus, bruised for our offences,
Heart of Jesus, obedient unto death,
Heart of Jesus, pierced with a lance,
Heart of Jesus, source of all consolation,
Heart of Jesus, our life and resurrection,
Heart of Jesus, our peace and reconciliation,
Heart of Jesus, victim for sin,
Heart of Jesus, salvation of those who trust in you,
Heart of Jesus, hope of those who die in you,
Heart of Jesus, delight of all saints,
Lamb of God, who takes away the sins of the world: *Spare us, O Lord.*
Lamb of God, who takes away the sins of the world: *Graciously hear us, O Lord.*
Lamb of God, who takes away the sins of the world: *Have mercy on us, O Lord.*

V. Jesus, meek and humble of Heart:

R. Make our hearts like unto Thine.

Let us pray

O ALMIGHTY and eternal God, look upon the Heart of your dearly beloved Son, and upon the praise and satisfaction he offers you in the name of sinners and of those who seek your mercy; be appeased, and grant us pardon in the name of the same Jesus Christ, your Son; who lives and reigns with you forever. Amen.

The Litany of Loreto

Lord, have mercy.
Lord, have mercy.
Christ, have mercy.
Christ, have mercy.
Lord, have mercy.
Lord, have mercy.
Christ, hear us.
Christ, graciously hear us.
God the Father of heaven, **have mercy on us.**
God the Son, Redeemer of the world,
God the Holy Spirit,
Holy Trinity, one God, Holy Mary, **pray for us.**
Holy Mother of God,
Holy Virgin of virgins, Mother of Christ,
Mother of divine grace,
Mother most pure,
Mother most chaste,
Mother inviolate, Mother undefiled, Mother most amiable,
Mother most admirable, Mother of good counsel, Mother of
our Creator, Mother of our Redeemer, Virgin most prudent,
Virgin most venerable, Virgin most renowned, Virgin most
powerful, Virgin most merciful, Virgin most faithful,
Mirror of justice, Seat of wisdom, Cause of our joy,
Spiritual vessel, Vessel of honor, Singular vessel of
devotion, Mystical rose, Tower of David, Tower of ivory,
House of gold, Ark of the covenant, Gate of heaven,
Morning star, Health of the sick, Refuge of sinners,
Comforter of the afflicted, Help of Christians, Queen of
angels, Queen of patriarchs, Queen of prophets, Queen of
apostles, Queen of martyrs, Queen of confessors, Queen of

virgins, Queen of all saints, Queen conceived without original sin, Queen of the most holy rosary, Lamb of God, who takes away the sins of the world: *Spare us, O Lord.* Lamb of God, who takes away the sins of the world: *Graciously hear us, O Lord.*
Lamb of God, who takes away the sins of the world: *Have mercy on us, O Lord.*

V. Pray for us, O holy Mother of God:

R. That we may be made worthy of the promises of Christ.

Let us pray

GRANT, we beseech you, O Lord God, that we, your servants, may enjoy perpetual health of mind and body; and by the intercession of the Blessed Mary, ever Virgin, may be delivered from preset sorrow, and obtain eternal joy. Through Christ our Lord. Amen.

Litany of the Saints

LORD, have mercy.
Lord, have mercy.
Christ, have mercy.
Christ, have mercy.
Lord, have mercy.
Lord, have mercy.
Christ, hear us.
Christ, graciously hear us.
God the Father of heaven, ***have mercy on us.***
God the Son, Redeemer of the world, God the Holy Spirit,
Holy Trinity, one God,
Holy Mary, ***pray for us.***
Holy Mother of God, Holy Virgin of virgins, St. Michael,
St. Gabriel, St. Raphael, All you holy angels and
archangels, All you holy orders of blessed spirits, St. John
Baptist, St. Joseph, All you holy patriarchs and prophets,
St. Peter, St. Paul, St. Andrew, St. James, St. John, St.
Thomas, St. James, St. Philip, St. Bartholomew, St.
Matthew, St. Simon, St. Thaddaeus, St. Mathias, St.
Barnabas, St. Luke, St. Mark, All you holy apostles and
evangelists,
All you holy disciples of Our Lord, All you holy innocents,
St. Stephen, St. Lawrence, St. Vincent, SS. Fabian and
Sebastian, SS. John and Paul, SS. Cosmas and Damian, SS.
Gervaise and Protaise, All you holy martyrs,
St. Sylvester, St. Gregory, St. Ambrose, St. Augustine, St.
Jerome, St. Martin, St. Nicholas, All you holy bishops and
confessors, All you holy doctors, St. Anthony,
St. Benedict, St. Bernard, St. Dominic, St. Francis, All you
holy priests and clergy, pray for us.

All you holy monks and hermits, pray for us.
St. Mary Magdalen, St. Agatha, St. Lucy, St. Agnes, St. Cecilia, St. Catherine, St. Anastasia, All you holy virgins and widows, All you men and women, saints of God,
Be merciful: *Spare us, O Lord.*
Be merciful: *Graciously hear us, O Lord.*
From all evil, **O Lord, deliver us.**
From all sin,
From a sudden and unforeseen death, From the snares of the devil, From anger, hatred, and ill will, From the spirit of fornication, From lightning and tempest,
From the scourge of earthquake,
From pestilence, famine, and war,
From everlasting death,
Through the mystery of your holy incarnation,
Through your coming,
Through your nativity,
Through your baptism and holy fasting,
Through your cross and passion,
Through your death and burial,
Through your holy resurrection,
Through your admirable ascension,
Through the coming of the Holy Spirit, the Comforter,
On the Day of Judgment,
We sinners ask you, *hear us.*
That you will spare us,
That you will pardon us,
That it may please you to bring us to true penance,
To govern and preserve your holy Church,
To preserve our apostolic prelate and all ecclesiastical orders in holy religion,
To humble the enemies of your holy Church,
To give peace and true concord to Christian kings and princes,

To grant peace and unity to all Christian people,
To confirm and preserve us in your holy service,
To raise our minds to heavenly desires,
To reward all our benefactors with eternal blessings,
To deliver our souls and those of our brethren, kinsfolk,
and benefactors from eternal damnation,
To give and preserve the fruits of the earth,
To grant eternal rest to all the faithful departed,
That it may please you to hear us, Son of the living God,

Lamb of God, who takes away the sins of the world: *Spare us, O Lord.*
Lamb of God, who takes away the sins of the world:
Graciously hear us, O Lord.
Lamb of God, who takes away the sins of the world: *Have mercy on us, O Lord.*

Christ, hear us.
Christ, graciously hear us.

Lord, have mercy.
Lord, have mercy.
Christ, have mercy.
Christ, have mercy.
Lord, have mercy.
Lord, have mercy.

REFERENCES/SUGGESTIONS FOR FURTHER READING:

Abrahams, Israel. 2007. *Encyclopedia Judaica*, 2nd ed., s.v. Prayer: In the Bible. Detroit: Thomson/Gale.

Arbesmann, R. 2003. *New Catholic Encyclopedia*, 2nd ed., s.v. Prayer. Detroit: Thomson/Gale.

Aumann, J. 2003. *New Catholic Encyclopedia*, 2nd ed., s.v. Contemplation. Detroit: Thomson/Gale.

Benedict of Nursia. 1982. *The Rule of St. Benedict in English*. Edited by Timothy Fry, O.S.B. Collegeville, MN: The Liturgical Press.

Benedict XVI (Joseph Ratzinger). 2007. Origen of Alexandria: The Thought (2). http://www.vatican.va/holy_father/benedict_xvi/audiences/2007/documents/hf_ben-xvi_aud_20070502_en.html (accessed February 8, 2014).

———. 2004. *Introduction to Christianity*. Translated by J. Foster. Revised edition. San Francisco: Ignatius.

———. 2000. *The Spirit of the Liturgy*. Translated by John Saward. San Francisco: Ignatius.

———. 1988. *Eschatology: Death and Eternal Life*. Translated by Michael Waldstein. Edited by Aidan Nichols, O.P. 2nd edition. Washington, DC: The Catholic University of America Press.

———. 1986. *The Feast of Faith: Approaches to a Theology of the Liturgy*. Translated by Graham Harrison. San Francisco: Ignatius.

Catholic Church. 1995. *Catechism of the Catholic Church.* Translated by United States Catholic Conference of Bishops. New York: Image.

———. *The Basic Sixteen Documents: Vatican Council II: Constitutions, Decrees, Declarations.* Edited by Austin Flannery, O.P. Northport, NY: Costello.

Charlesworth, James H. 1992. Prayer in Early Judaism. *The Anchor Bible Dictionary.* New York: Doubleday.

Dionysius the Areopagite. 2004. *The Mystical Theology and The Divine Names.* Translated by C.E. Rolt. New York: Dover.

Escrivá, Josemaría. 1982. *The Way.* New York: Scepter.

Francis de Sales. 2002. *Introduction to the Devout Life.* New York: Vintage Spiritual Classics.

Griffin, Emilie, ed. 1981. *The Cloud of Unknowing.* New York: Harper Collins.

Guigo II. 1978. *The Ladder of Monks and Twelve Meditations.* Translated by Edmund Colledge, O.S.A. and James Walsh, S.J. New York: Image.

Hourlier, Jacques. 2004. *Reflections on the Spirituality of Gregorian Chant.* Translated by Gregory Casprini and Robert Edmonson. Revised edition. Orleans, MA: Paraclete Press.

Ignatius of Loyola. 1964. *The Spiritual Exercises of St. Ignatius.* Translated by Anthony Mottola. New York: Image.

John of the Cross. 1979. *The Collected Works of St. John of the Cross.* Translated by Kieran Kavanaugh, O.C.D. and Otilio Rodriguez, O.C.D. Washington, DC: ICS Publications.

Kennedy, D., and M. B. Pennington. 2003. *New Catholic Encyclopedia*, 2nd ed., s.v. Prayer (Theology of). Detroit: Thomson/Gale.

Mastermann, M. R. E. 2003. *New Catholic Encyclopedia*, 2nd ed., s.v. Prayer (In the Bible). Detroit: Thomson/Gale.

Montfort, Louis Mary de. 1993. *The Secret of the Rosary*. Translated by Mary Barbour, T.O.P. Rockford, IL: Tan.

Palmer, P.F., and G. A. Tavardi. 2003. *New Catholic Encyclopedia*, 2nd ed., s.v. Indulgences. Detroit: Thomson/Gale.

Saulnier, Daniel. 2003. *Gregorian Chant: A Guide*. Translated by Edward Schaefer. La Froidfontaine, France: Solesmes.

Tanquerey, Adolphe. 2000. *The Spiritual Life: A Treatise on Ascetical and Mystical Theology*. Translated by Herman Branderis, S.S., A.M. 2nd edition. Rockford, IL: Tan.

Theresa of Ávila. 2004. *Interior Castle*. Translated and edited by E. Allison Peers. New York: Image.

Thérèse of Lisieux. 1996. *Story of a Soul: The Autobiography of St. Thérèse of Lisieux*. Translated by John Clark, O.C.D. 3rd edition. Washington, DC: ICS Publications.

www.ingramcontent.com/pod-product-compliance
Lightning Source LLC
Chambersburg PA
CBHW071458070426
42452CB00041B/1924